100 KILLER RIFFS & FILLS FOR ROCK GUITAR

100 KILLER RIFFS & FILLS FOR ROCK GUITAR

ALL THE HOT RIFFS & FILLS YOU NEED—AND HOW TO USE THEM

PHIL CAPONE

CHARTWELL
BOOKS, INC.

This edition published in 2012 by Chartwell Books, Inc.,
A division of Book Sales, Inc.
276 Fifth Avenue Suite 206
New York, NY 10001
USA

ISBN: 978-0-7858–2891-4
QTT.HKRF

A Quintet Book
Copyright © 2012 Quintet Publishing Limited
All rights reserved.

This book was conceived, designed, and produced by
Quintet Publishing Limited
The Old Brewery
6 Blundell Street
London N7 9BH
United Kingdom

Senior Editor: Ruth Patrick
Designer: Rod Teasdale
Art Director: Michael Charles
Editorial Director: Donna Gregory
Publisher: Mark Searle

Printed in China by Midas Printing International Ltd.

9 8 7 6 5 4 3 2 1

Author's web site: caponeguitar.com

CONTENTS

INTRODUCTION

This book has been written with just one objective in mind: to turn you into a proficient rock guitarist. It achieves this through an in-depth analysis of the six most important styles in rock today—blues rock, classic rock, heavy metal, prog rock, alternative rock, and fusion. You'll study riffs and fills presented in the style of the legendary players from each of these subgenres. Work through this book and you'll be a vastly different player by the time you've finished it; fully "schooled up" and ready to rock like a pro.

Designed as a companion to *100 Killer Licks & Chops for Rock Guitar*, this book reveals the tricks of the trade used by all the great rock guitarists. As you progress through the book, not only will you build your musical vocabulary, but you'll also develop a skill set enabling you to create your own killer riffs and fills. You'll learn riffs designed to work in a specific section of a song (i.e., intro, verse, or chorus), which will help to make your own riffs more focused and effective. The art of playing tasteful fills is also clearly explained—again with a clear indication of where, how, and why they would be used.

You don't need to be a guitar whizz to use this book, but it is assumed that you have a functional level of ability. Hopefully, players of all levels will find it a useful and informative resource. Because this is not a traditional "teach yourself" book, it is not progressive—that's to say, it can be dipped into at any point, whenever inspiration or just some fresh ideas are needed. All of the licks and riffs are demonstrated on the accompanying CD, so don't be put off by "the dots." As long as you can read TAB (and we've even included an explanation, in case you can't), you'll be able to play everything in this book. To help you to max up your technique and increase your knowledge of the fingerboard, an extensive "chops builder" section follows the lick chapters.

Of course, there are many guitar books and DVDs on the market today, but this one is genuinely unique. It illustrates the stylistic approaches of as many pioneering guitarists as we could squeeze in, from 1960s blues rock to fusion. As well as learning killer riffs and fills, you'll also learn how each genre evolved, and the book provides you with a comprehensive history of rock guitar as you play. So what are you waiting for? Crank up that amp—let's rock!

HOW TO USE THIS BOOK

KILLER RIFFS AND FILLS

These boxes provide essential information on technique, as well as suggesting when to use each riff or fill.

Play the relevant track on the CD to hear how the riffs and fills should sound.

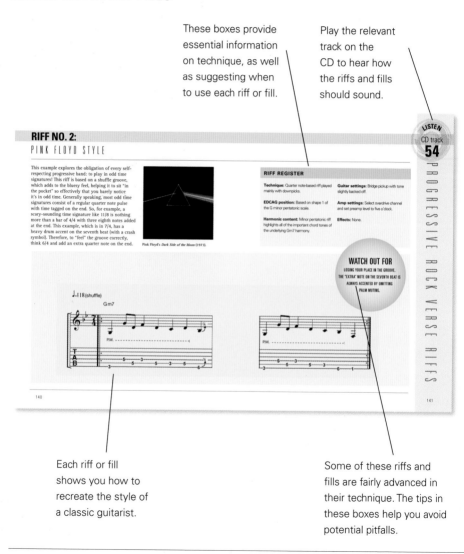

RIFF NO. 2:

PINK FLOYD STYLE

LISTEN
CD track
54

PROGRESSIVE ROCK VERSE RIFFS

This example explores the obligation of every self-respecting progressive band: to play in odd time signatures! This riff is based on a shuffle groove, which adds to the bluesy feel, helping it to sit "in the pocket" so effectively that you barely notice it's in odd time. Generally speaking, most odd time signatures consist of a regular quarter note pulse with time tagged on the end. So, for example, a scary-sounding time signature like 11/8 is nothing more than a bar of 4/4 with three eighth notes added at the end. This example, which is in 7/4, has a heavy drum accent on the seventh beat (with a crash symbol). Therefore, to "feel" the groove correctly, think 6/4 and add an extra quarter note on the end.

Pink Floyd's *Dark Side of the Moon* (1973).

RIFF REGISTER

Technique: Quarter note-based riff played mainly with downpicks.

EDCAG position: Based on shape 1 of the G minor pentatonic scale.

Harmonic content: Minor pentatonic riff highlights all of the important chord tones of the underlying Gm7 harmony.

Guitar settings: Bridge pickup with tone slightly backed off.

Amp settings: Select overdrive channel and set preamp level to five o'clock.

Effects: None.

WATCH OUT FOR
LOSING YOUR PLACE IN THE GROOVE. THE "EXTRA" NOTE ON THE SEVENTH BEAT IS ALWAYS ACCENTED BY OMITTING PALM MUTING.

♩=118 (shuffle)
Gm7

140

141

Each riff or fill shows you how to recreate the style of a classic guitarist.

Some of these riffs and fills are fairly advanced in their technique. The tips in these boxes help you avoid potential pitfalls.

SCALES AND CHOPS

The scales and chops section is the "technique busting" part of the book designed to advance your playing skills. Instead of just ascending and descending stepwise scale patterns, these challenging exercises will prepare you for "real world" improvisation scenarios.

SCALES AND CHOPS
DORIAN MODE WORKOUT

Ex 1 Diatonic thirds (shape one)

Ex 2 Diatonic 4-note arpeggios (shape one)

(economy picking shown)

228

229

DORIAN MODE WORKOUT

Each exercise is presented clearly and concisely using conventional notation and TAB. Helpful fingering suggestions are also provided to eliminate awkward or clumsy hand movements.

Learning the various forms of notation will make you a more versatile musician.

GUITAR NOTATION

The CAGED system is a beautifully conceived philosophy that rationalizes the guitar's fretboard. Once you start using it, you'll wonder how you ever managed without it! All the pros use the CAGED system, which organizes the guitar's fretboard into five distinct zones or shapes. The shape used for each zone remains constant in every key (but moves to a different fret), and can be applied to chords, arpeggios, scale patterns, and riffs or licks. Basically, if you can play it, then it can be CAGED. The system also provides an excellent model for practice: by practicing new material in each of the five shapes, transposing it to other keys will become a breeze.

The second section of this chapter fully explains how to read TAB, the most widely used system of guitar notation, which is used throughout this book. You're probably already a proficient TAB reader, but all of the symbols for bends, slurs, and vibratos are included here as a convenient reference, just in case you need them. There's no explanation of the conventional notation here, it would be beyond the scope of this book. However if you can't read traditional music yet, don't panic, the combination of CD and TAB alone is really all you need. You'll also find that by the time you've worked through this book your sight-reading skills will have improved considerably. Lastly, you'll find a full explanation of the Nashville Numbering System that's used to describe the harmonic setting of each riff, lick, and fill.

THE CAGED SYSTEM
THE CAGED OPEN POSITION SHAPES

"CAGED" is an acronym for those five open major chord shapes that every fledgling guitarist takes their first steps with. In case you haven't played them for a while, here's a reminder:

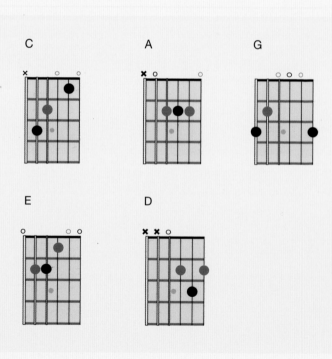

CAGED SHAPES IN C

To achieve the CAGED mapping system, the five
shapes need to be transposed into the same key
(e.g., C major) and then converted to moveable
shapes. They can then be placed end to end along
the fretboard (spelling "CAGED"), covering the
entire neck in five different C chord shapes:

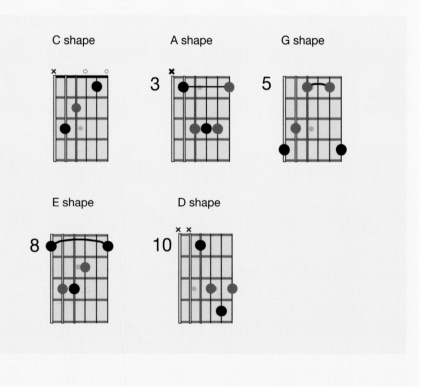

THE CAGED SYSTEM
EDCAG SHAPES IN F

Because the "E shape" pattern has its root note on the sixth string, it makes sense to use this as the starting point for the CAGED system and to call it "shape 1," to avoid any confusion when transposing. This results in a reorganized system that spells "EDCAG." The system now begins with shape 1 and ascends to shape 5 (in any key). Guitarists still refer to this model as the CAGED system, even though the order of the patterns has been changed. The lowest possible position for a full six-string barre chord is on the first fret, i.e., an F chord. In the example below, you can clearly see the interlocking five shapes of the EDCAG system in the key of F.

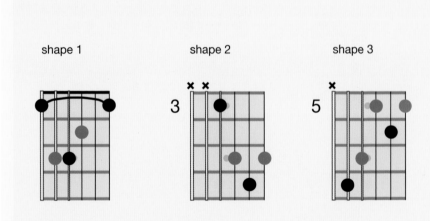

EDCAG in this book

The CAGED system is used throughout this book, both in the riffs and fills and the riff builder sections. To avoid confusion, reference to the original open chord shape has been dropped in preference to an EDCAG numerical reference (e.g., shape 1, shape 4). This is common practice in education establishments and guitar publications worldwide.

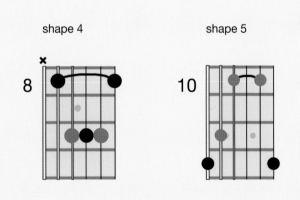

shape 4

shape 5

READING TAB

"TAB" is short for "tablature," a simplified system of notation that's widely used for guitar. Many people wrongly assume that this is a modern system, and was born in the age of the internet. In fact, it dates back to the Renaissance period (c. 1400–1600), when it was used to notate music for the lute. Today it's used in music publications worldwide, and is the most common form of guitar notation. TAB uses six lines (called a stave), each one symbolizing one of the guitar's six strings. Numbers are written on the lines to indicate the frets played. It's as simple as that!

You can see how the six strings of the guitar are represented in TAB form in example 1. Remember: the sixth string is the lowest!

Hammer-ons and pull-offs are indicated by a bracket between the two notes (example 2). Pick the first note only–the second pitch is created by firmly fretting the higher note (hammer on) or flicking your fretting finger sideways as you release it (pull off).

Ex1 The open strings

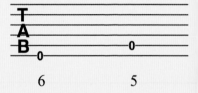

Ex2 Hammer-ons and pull-offs

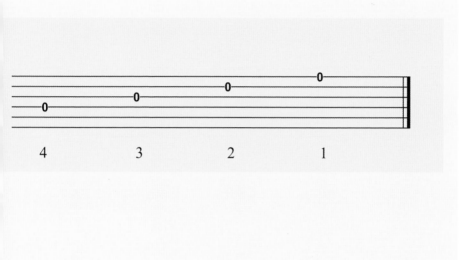

4   3   2   1

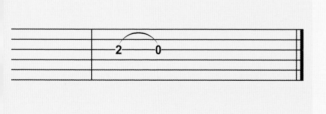

READING TAB

Slides (example 3) are indicated by a straight line in two ways—either between two different pitches on the same string or as a "tail" that falls away from a single note or chord. When drawn between two pitches, pick only the first note and slide up (or down) the fretboard to the second note without removing your finger from the string. When drawn after a note or chord, the line indicates a slide down the neck from the given fret (the player can freely interpret how far the slide should travel).

String bends (example 4) are achieved by fretting the first note, and then bending up to the virtual pitch that's indicated by the symbol above the bend arrow (see Bending box). Bend and release simply involves a release back to the original pitch (in brackets). A pre-bend release involves bending the string to the fret indicated, picking the note, and then releasing it to its normal pitch, as shown in brackets.

Vibrato (example 5) is always indicated by a single wavy line above a note. Some blues players (most notably B. B. King and Eric Clapton) execute vibrato with their thumb off the neck, which intensifies the effect. When it's required, this will be mentioned in the accompanying text.

Ex3 Slides

Ex4 String Bends

1) whole step bend

Ex5 Vibrato

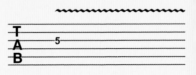

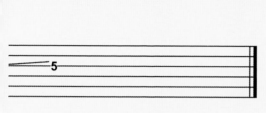

Bending legend

¼ = quarter tone
(less than one fret) bend

½ = half step
(one fret) bend

Full = whole step
(two frets) bend

1½ = one and a half step
(three frets) bend

2 = two whole steps
(four frets) bend

2) half step bend & release   3) whole step pre-bend release

READING TAB

Trills (example 6) are created by a brisk oscillation with a note that's either a whole step or half step above. These are generally not written rhythmically. Instead, they're indicated with the higher note indicated in brackets in the TAB (see illustration). Pick only the first note, and use consecutive hammer-ons and pull-offs to create the trill effect.

Ex6 Trills

1) whole step trill

```
    tr~~~~~~~~~~~~~~~~~~~~~~~
T|----------------------------
A|-7-(9)----------------------
B|----------------------------
```

Two-handed tapping (example 7) is used to create impressive legato passages. Pitches are created by tapping the first finger of your picking hand on the fretboard of the guitar at the fret indicated in the TAB. The "T" indicates which notes should be tapped. Following pitches are generated by pulling off the finger to the fretted note. This is usually followed by a hammer-on, as shown in example 6.

2) half step trill

Ex7 Two-Handed Tapping

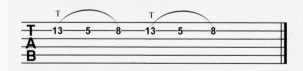

THE NASHVILLE NUMBERING SYSTEM

Professional musicians don't just view chords as being A7, G minor, or E. They think of the root notes as a sequence of intervals that relate to the tonic of the key they're playing in. This system makes for easy transposition, allowing a chord sequence to be played in any key, instantly. It also means that familiar chord sequences are instantly recognizable (e.g., turnarounds, cadences, or entire progressions like a 12-bar blues), which is particularly useful when improvising.

Tune in!

Pros can identify chord sequences without their instrument just by listening. This doesn't require perfect pitch (the majority of musicians do not possess this skill)—just a highly developed ear. It's a great tool to possess and can be learned over time, just like any other skill. Next time you hear a tune on the radio, concentrate on the bass line. Once you can identify the root movement of a chord progression, filling in the details (whether the chord is major, minor, or a dominant seventh) should be easy.

Romans to Nashville

When notating an interval-based chord sequence, Roman numerals are always used. This is an established harmonic convention that was first used in classical music in conjunction with the figured bass system. In the 1950s, the system was simplified and adopted by the Nashville session musicians of the day—hence its name. Therefore, a 12-bar blues would be described as a I, IV, V sequence, because it contains chords built on the tonic (I), the perfect fourth (IV), and the perfect fifth (V). It's exactly the same as describing the intervals of a scale. Below, the minor pentatonic is first described as a scale formula (indicating the intervals of the scale) and then in Roman numerals (describing a minor pentatonic chord sequence). Accidentals are necessary in both scenarios.

Minor pentatonic: $1 - \flat3 - 4 - 5 - \flat7$

Minor pentatonic chord progression:
$I - \flat III - IV - V - \flat VII$

THE ROMAN NUMERAL SYSTEM

Basic 12-bar blues

Here's how the Nashville Numbering System relates to the chords of a basic 12-bar blues. The chord symbols are limited to the key of C, whereas the numbers can be applied to any key. Because it's understood that all the chords in the progression are dominant sevenths, there's no need to add a "7" after each number.

Fig1 Basic 12-bar blues

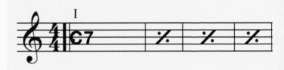

Complex 12-bar blues

More complex "changes" (a term that musos use to describe chord progressions) may add a quick change in bar 2, a diminished chord in bar 6, and a "turnaround" in bars 11 and 12. This is how a more complex chord sequence would be written with chord symbols (again in C major) and as Nashville Numbering. Notice that non-diatonic chords (i.e., chords that contain notes outside of the key) are always qualified when they occur (hence F#° is written as #IV° and A7 as VI7).

Fig2 Complex 12-bar blues

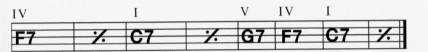

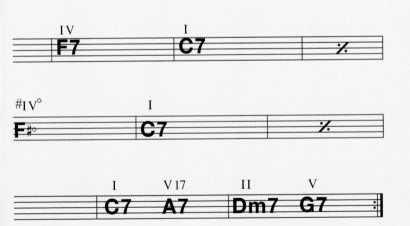

Blues rock virtuoso Joe Bonamassa of Black Country Communion performs at the City National Grove of Anaheim in June 2011.

10 KILLER BLUES ROCK ALBUMS YOU CAN'T AFFORD TO IGNORE

1 *John Mayall Blues Breakers with Eric Clapton*
   • (aka *The Beano Album*) (1966)
2 Cream • *Disraeli Gears* (1967)
3 Led Zeppelin • *Led Zeppelin II* (1969)
4 Free • *Fire and Water* (1970)
5 Allman Brothers Band • *At Fillmore East* (1971)
6 Mountain • *Nantucket Sleighride* (1971)
7 Rory Gallagher • *Live in Europe* (1972)
8 Stevie Ray Vaughan • *Texas Flood* (1983)
9 Gary Moore • *Still Got the Blues* (1990)
10 Joe Bonamassa • *Sloe Gin* (2007)

BLUES ROCK

The blues rock movement was inspired by the Chicago blues musicians of the 1940s and 1950s. At this time in the United States, there was a huge migration from the Mississippi Delta and the southern States to northern cities such as Chicago. Because the Windy City was the industrial capital of the country, there was plenty of work for those who were willing to make the journey. Armed with electric guitars and amplifiers, the new breed of "work by day, play by night" blues musicians revolutionized the sound of the blues. It was no longer an acoustic music played by solo performers; the blues band was born. Lineups were very similar to today's groups—drums, bass, guitar, piano, and vocals.

English musicians in the early 1960s were unable to compete with the relentless stream of rock and roll acts from the States, and were searching for a sound of their own. They took their inspiration from the American blues musicians instead—specifically, those from Chicago—so, ironically, the unlikely champions of the blues were white English, middle-class, ex-art-school students such as Eric Clapton, Jeff Beck, and Jimmy Page. They not only sold the blues back to the United States, but also revived the careers of many of its native blues musicians.

The genre continued to evolve into the 1970s. The 12-bar form became less relevant, but the minimalist approach, locked grooves, cool guitar tone, and heavily blues-influenced solos remained central to the music's philosophy. Pioneers included players like Paul Kossoff, Rory Gallagher, and Leslie West. By the 1980s, the music business was changing fast and the mantle was handed over to those who were prepared to embrace the new MTV phenomenon—among them, Gary Moore, Stevie Ray Vaughan, Jeff Healey, and Billy Gibbons. In recent years, the emergence of talented new blues rock virtuosos such as Joe Bonamassa, Derek Trucks, Walter Trout, and Seasick Steve proves that blues rock is very much alive and well in the 21st century.

RIFF NO. 1:
PAUL KOSSOFF STYLE

One of rock music's most underrated guitar players, the late Paul Kossoff was the driving force behind 1970s blues rock pioneers Free. He was also the man responsible for the iconic riff in the band's 1970 single release "All Right Now." The song was a huge hit for the group and still receives heavy airplay on rock radio stations to this day. The example given here is typical of Kossoff's approach: big, resonant, sustained open chord voicings contrasted with snappier triad-based phrases, all played against a constant tonic bass note pedal. Typically, this type of riff would be used to set the vibe in a song's intro, but it could also be reused as the chorus or as an interlude riff later in the arrangement.

Paul Kossoff performing in London in 1975.

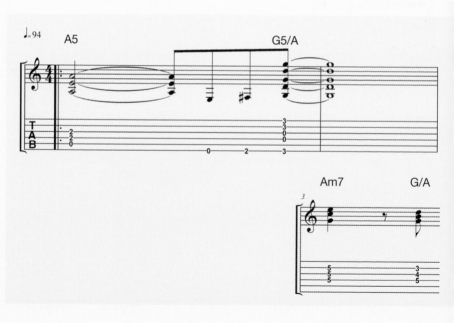

RIFF REGISTER

Technique: Played pickstyle, so open strings need to be carefully damped when they're not part of the chord.

EDCAG position: Open shape 4 A chord and shape 5 G chord.

Harmonic content: Tonic power chord followed by a ♭VII chord (G5) superimposed against a tonic bass note creating Mixolydian flavors.

Guitar settings: Bridge pickup, with tone control backed off slightly to "warm up" the sound.

Amp settings: Select overdrive channel, keeping preamp settings at around five o'clock.

Effects: None.

WATCH OUT FOR

ACCIDENTALLY SOUNDING THE NOTES ON HIGHER STRINGS WHEN BARRING ACROSS THE SECOND FRET TO PLAY THE A5 CHORD.

RIFF NO. 2:
BILLY GIBBONS STYLE

Billy Gibbons is a blues rock virtuoso. As guitarist and frontman for that hard-rocking "Little Ole' Band from Texas," he knows a thing or two about killer riffs! ZZ Top (it's pronounced "zee zee") have been selling records and rocking audiences since the early 1970s. They have released 14 albums to date, achieving impressive gold, platinum, and multi-platinum sales worldwide. The key to Billy's appeal is that he never wastes a note; his intensely musical and minimalist style has kept ZZ Top in rock's first division for more than four decades. This example illustrates his style perfectly. It's an infectious riff created from just four notes of the G minor pentatonic scale (G, F, B♭, and C).

ZZ Top performing in the United States.

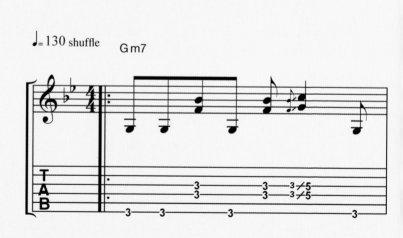

B L U E S   R O C K   I N T R O   R I F F S

RIFF REGISTER

Technique: Use alternate eighth note picking throughout. Hybrid picking can also be used for a smoother alternation between bass notes and double stops.

EDCAG position: Shape 1 G minor pentatonic scale.

Harmonic content: Double-stop riff using diatonic fourths from the G minor pentatonic scale.

Guitar settings: Bridge pickup, volume up full for fat tone.

Amp settings: Select overdrive channel, set preamp level at around seven o'clock.

Effects: None.

WATCH OUT FOR

MOVING SWIFTLY BETWEEN THE BASS NOTES AND DOUBLE STOPS WITH YOUR FRETTING HAND. USE THE FINGERING INDICATED FOR BEST RESULTS.

B♭5

RIFF NO. 3:
MICK RALPHS STYLE

When Free split in 1973, singer Paul Rodgers formed Bad Company with ex-Mott the Hoople guitarist Mick Ralphs. The band has recorded some of the most memorable and infectious blues rock songs in the genre's history, all underpinned by the stellar guitar work of Mr. Ralphs. Like all blues rock virtuosos, he completely understands the importance of minimalism and making every note count. By never playing anything flashy or ostentatious, his musical approach is the perfect example of "It's not what you play, but what you leave out"! This example typifies his preference for power-chord-based riffs that create a full, powerful sound.

Mick Ralphs performing in 1979.

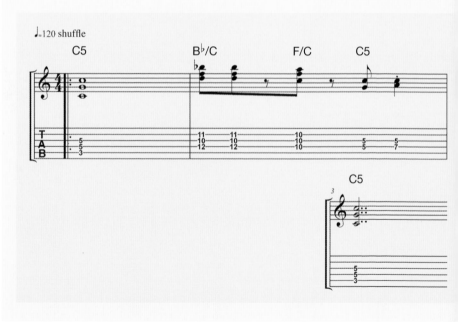

RIFF REGISTER

Technique: Pickstyle using downstrokes throughout to allow natural accenting of the off beat power chords.

EDCAG position: Shape 4 power chord mixed with shape 3 (B♭) and shape 5 (F) triads.

Harmonic content: Tonic power chord in the first bar moves into gospel-flavored IV/I territory in the second bar.

Guitar settings: Bridge and neck pickup, volume backed off slightly to "tame" the overdrive.

Amp settings: Select overdrive channel, set preamp level to around eight o'clock.

Effects: None.

WATCH OUT FOR

OBSERVING THE RESTS IN THE SECOND BAR. TO DAMP THE CHORDS, RELEASE THE PRESSURE OF YOUR FRETTING HAND SLIGHTLY.

E♭5   B♭5

RIFF NO. 4:

ERIC CLAPTON STYLE

During the 1960s, Cream enjoyed a brief but prolific reign as the world's first supergroup. Eric Clapton, Ginger Baker, and Jack Bruce established blues rock as the coolest of rock genres. The powerhouse trio set the blueprint that countless bands would imitate but seldom equal. In this example, a simple, yet effective riff creates a sense of urgency and expectation by implying a double-time feel during the song's intro. This heavily syncopated style owes a debt to the pioneering work of Chicago bluesman Bo Diddley. Bo was the first bluesman to ditch the 12-bar form and base his songs on riffs alone. His riffing style was a big influence on the early blues rock pioneers, including the young Eric Clapton.

Eric Clapton at Atlantic Studios in 1967.

RIFF REGISTER

Technique: Alternate sixteenth note strumming throughout.

EDCAG position: Full shape 1, six-string barre chords.

Harmonic content: Diatonic (E, A) and non-diatonic (G, D) major chords are mixed together to create a bluesy, harmonically ambiguous sound.

Guitar settings: Neck pickup, tone on full to avoid a muddy, indistinct sound.

Amp settings: Select overdrive channel, set preamp level to around three o'clock.

Effects: None.

WATCH OUT FOR

MOVING THAT BIG CHORD SHAPE QUICKLY AROUND THE NECK! TRY FRETTING THE OPEN E CHORD USING YOUR SECOND, THIRD, AND FOURTH FINGERS TO FACILITATE A QUICK CHANGE TO THE FULL G BARRE.

RIFF NO. 1:

JIMMY PAGE STYLE

Jimmy Page needs little introduction. His work with Led Zeppelin spanned three decades, a body of work that has influenced just about every rock musician on the planet. In addition to cutting his teeth with the Yardbirds, Page was also one of the busiest session guitarists on the London scene in the 1960s. All this recording experience paid off when he formed Led Zeppelin from the ashes of the Yardbirds. His pioneering approach involved creating a rich tapestry of sound by layering multi-tracked guitar parts. By using acoustic guitar for the verse, as this "Zep-style" riff does, an instant contrast can be created with heavier electric sounds on the chorus.

Jimmy Page performing on stage.

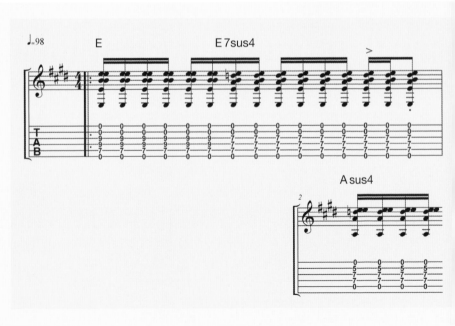

RIFF REGISTER

Technique: Strummed acoustic guitar part using alternate sixteenth note picking.

EDCAG position: Shape 4 power chord followed by shape 1 and three major triads.

Harmonic content: Tonic power chord mixed with triads IV and ♭VII sounded against open strings.

Guitar settings: Maintain a light but constant sixteenth note strumming pattern to achieve a warm, percussive acoustic tone.

Amp settings: Not applicable.

Effects: None.

WATCH OUT FOR

THAT TRICKY E7 SUS4 SHAPE THAT INVOLVES A PARTIAL BARRE WITH THE FIRST FINGER. TAKE CARE NOT TO DAMP THE FIRST AND SECOND STRINGS, WHICH MUST BE ALLOWED TO RING THROUGHOUT.

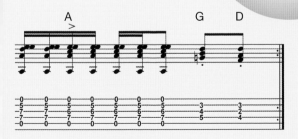

RIFF NO. 2:
ANGUS YOUNG STYLE

Angus Young's career with AC/DC began in the early 1970s. The Aussie rockers have notched up an incredible string of platinum, gold, and silver album sales over the last four decades, so Mr. Young certainly knows a thing or two about writing killer riffs. This example illustrates his no-nonsense, hard-hitting style and is typical of his approach to verse riffs: simple, driving, and effective. To add weight in the chorus sections, a riff like this would typically be doubled or played higher up the neck (often as inversions) by Angus's brother, Malcolm.

Angus Young performing in 1986.

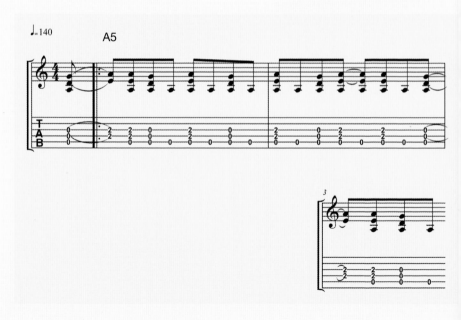

RIFF REGISTER

Technique: Although this riff has a bright tempo, use downpicks to achieve a more driving groove.

EDCAG position: Open shape 4 tonic power chord. Shape 2 (D/F#) and five (G) major chords provide contrast in the last bar.

Harmonic content: By mixing the open third and fourth strings with the regular A5 chord shape, the riff adds A11 (G/A) sounds into the mix.

Guitar settings: Bridge pickup, with volume and tone up full.

Amp settings: Select overdrive channel, set preamp level high, and play as loud as you dare!

Effects: None.

WATCH OUT FOR

KEEP THE RIFF SOUNDING TIGHT
AND MEAN: TRY ADDING SUBTLE
PALM MUTING WITH YOUR
PICKING HAND.

RIFF NO. 3:
JEFF BECK STYLE

Like Jimmy Page and Eric Clapton, Jeff Beck was also a member of the Yardbirds during the 1960s. After quitting the group, he formed his own band, the Jeff Beck Group, with Rod Stewart on vocals. The band's first album, *Truth* (1968), was a blues rock tour de force. This verse riff illustrates how immersed in the blues Beck was at this point in his career, as later albums would take a much jazzier direction. This example is a classic 12/8 shuffle style riff given the Jeff Beck treatment by adding a couple of twists—the major sixth (G#) in the first bar and the use of the D5 and A5 power chords in the fourth bar.

Jeff Beck performing in the United States in 1976.

RIFF REGISTER

Technique: Played pickstyle.

EDCAG position: Shape 1 B minor pentatonic scale. G# is added from shape 2 of the major pentatonic, while the low D on the fifth string is "borrowed" from shape 5 of the minor pentatonic.

Harmonic content: A typically ambiguous blues riff that never states the major third (D#) of the key.

Guitar settings: Neck pickup; back off volume to "tame" overdrive sound.

Amp settings: Select overdrive channel, set preamp level on full, and use your guitar volume to "clean up" the sound.

Effects: None.

WATCH OUT FOR

THE SLIDE ON THE FIFTH STRING AT THE END OF THE FIRST BAR. START THE SLIDE ON YOUR THIRD FINGER, AS THIS LEAVES YOUR FIRST FINGER FREE TO PLAY THE TONIC NOTE THAT FOLLOWS ON THE FOURTH STRING.

RIFF NO. 4:

JOE BONAMASSA STYLE

Although Joe Bonamassa is still regarded as a "newcomer" in the blues rock world, at the time of writing he already had an incredible 13 solo albums under his belt. Not only were both of Joe's parents musicians, but they also owned a guitar shop. No surprise, then, that he started playing guitar at just 4 years of age, and could play Stevie Ray Vaughan and Jimi Hendrix solos note for note by the time he was 7! Bonamassa has a real knack for writing the "riffs that got away," and this example is typical of his style. Part Clapton, part Mick Ralphs, and part Jimmy Page, it's an exciting mix of influences that sounds both fresh and new and true to the blues rock style.

Joe Bonamassa performing in 2011.

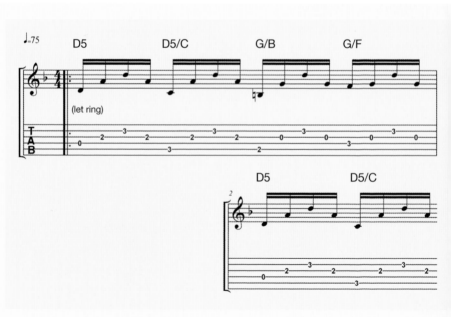

RIFF REGISTER

Technique: Alternate or economy sixteenth-note picking can be used.

EDCAG position: Open D5, G, Gm, and C chord shapes in first position.

Harmonic content: High tonic pedal note (D) is sounded throughout, with shifting bass pattern creating a hypnotic, bluesy riff.

Guitar settings: Position 2 on a Strat, or middle position on a guitar with two pickups.

Amp settings: Select clean channel, and adjust treble to prevent tone from being too bright.

Effects: Rotary speaker pedal or chorus effect to emulate the sound of a guitar played through a Leslie cabinet.

WATCH OUT FOR

MAINTAINING A CONSTANT SIXTEENTH NOTE PICKING RHYTHM WITHOUT LOSING THE GROOVE WHEN CHANGING SHAPES.

Gm/B♭   Csus2

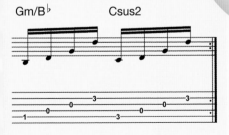

RIFF NO. 1:
KEITH RICHARDS STYLE

You may think the Rolling Stones are an odd choice for typifying the blues rock genre, but back in the early 1960s they were on the cutting edge of the British blues boom. The antithesis of the Beatles, they shunned matching suits, sharp haircuts, and happy pop songs in favor of scruffy jeans, long hair, and a healthy preference for R&B. Keith Richards is well known for his love of the blues and has frequently cited Muddy Waters, Bo Diddley, and Howlin' Wolf as major influences. This riff exemplifies Keith's approach in the early days of the band's career. His (for the time) dark-sounding blues riffs added texture and style to what would otherwise be a rather bland arrangement.

Keith Richards in 1967.

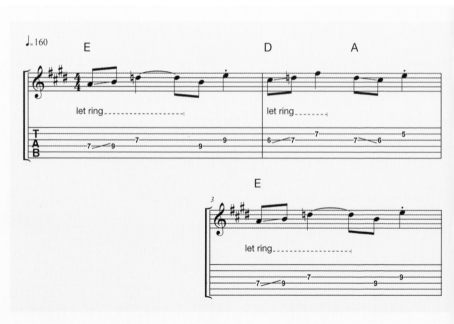

RIFF REGISTER

Technique: Single-note riff incorporating bluesy slides. A more muscular delivery can be achieved by playing it entirely with downpicks.

EDCAG position: Shape 4 E minor pentatonic scale.

Harmonic content: Note content from shape 4 of the E minor pentatonic

scale, with notes from the D and A chords added in the second bar.

Guitar settings: Neck pickup with volume and tone up full.

Amp settings: Clean channel with plenty of bass and middle for a fat tone.

Effects: Tremolo pedal.

WATCH OUT FOR

ALLOWING THE NOTES TO RING INTO EACH OTHER WHERE INDICATED. THIS IS AN IMPORTANT PART OF THE RIFF'S CHARACTERISTIC SOUND.

D   A

let ring

RIFF NO. 2:
LESLIE WEST STYLE

By the end of the 1960s, America was fighting against
the British invasion with its own brand of blues rock.
Spearheaded by bands such as Mountain, the Allman
Brothers, and Canned Heat, their sound was heavy, but with
well-crafted songs containing strong melodies. They laid
the foundations for the slick AOR rock sound that would
be dominating the American airwaves by the mid-1970s.
As Mountain's guitarist, vocalist, and frontman, Leslie West
was undoubtedly one of the pioneers of this new sound. This
example illustrates the big sound he achieved by crafting
riffs, from single notes and also three-note power chords.
This approach has remained central to rock music to this day.

Leslie West performing at Woodstock in 1969.

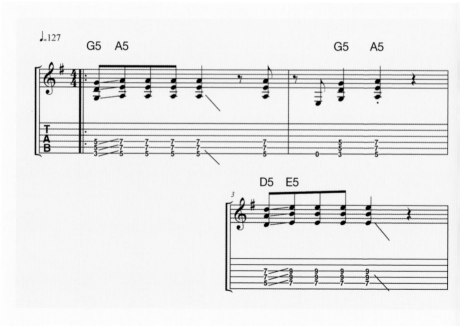

RIFF REGISTER

Technique: Use downpicks to play all of the power chords—this will create a more uniform, controlled tone.

EDCAG position: Shape 4 power chords mixed with a shape 3 minor pentatonic single note line.

Harmonic content: All of the chord and note content is diatonic to the E minor pentatonic scale.

Guitar settings: Bridge pickup with volume and tone up full.

Amp settings: Select distortion channel, and set preamp level to 5 o'clock.

Effects: None.

WATCH OUT FOR

KEEPING THE POWER CHORD SHAPES INTACT AS YOU SLIDE ALONG THE NECK.

N.C.

RIFF NO. 3:
STEVIE RAY VAUGHAN STYLE

The late Stevie Ray Vaughan hit the big time in the early 1980s, when "hair metal" bands and processed guitar sounds were in vogue. His raw, powerful brand of Texas blues sounded fresh and authentic. Heavily influenced by Jimi Hendrix, S. R. V. frequently featured the #9 chord (known by guitarists as "the Hendrix chord") in his compositions. This ambiguous-sounding chord simultaneously manages to be both major and minor, so it's perfect for blues rock. This example illustrates Stevie's knack for mixing single-note minor pentatonic riffs with #9 chord punctuations, creating a powerful rhythmic soundscape perfect for a powerhouse trio lineup.

Stevie Ray Vaughan performing in 1984.

RIFF REGISTER

Technique: Played pickstyle with alternate picking throughout.

EDCAG position: Shape 4 E7#9 chord mixed with shape 3 E minor pentatonic single-note riffs.

Harmonic content: A typically ambiguous blues riff that cleverly disguises its E major tonality.

Guitar settings: Position 4 on a Strat, or middle position on a two-pickup guitar.

Amp settings: Clean channel, but with amp cranked up loud to get those power tubes singing!

Effects: Rotary speaker simulator or chorus pedal to emulate Leslie cabinet.

WATCH OUT FOR

THE QUICK CHANGE FROM THE E7#9 CHORD TO THE LOW B NOTE ON THE SIXTH STRING. USE YOUR SECOND FINGER TO FRET THE B AND PLAY THE D THAT FOLLOWS WITH YOUR FIRST.

RIFF NO. 4:
GARY MOORE STYLE

Gary Moore was one of the UK's finest blues guitarists. As well as serving with Thin Lizzy and Colosseum II, he also enjoyed a successful solo career that began in 1973. As a solo artist his output was prolific, he released 20 albums in total. His most successful, the multi-platinum-selling *Still Got the Blues*, was released in 1990. Moore possessed a powerful blues voice, so he frequently toured with just a bassist and drummer as supporting musicians. As in this example, he would often underpin his chorus sections with powerful, fiery riffs, hitting the listener with an infectious "double hook."

Gary Moore performing in 2009.

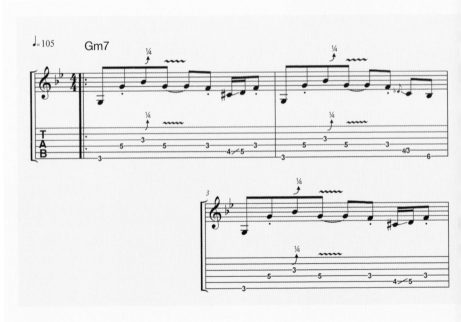

BLUES ROCK CHORUS RIFFS

RIFF REGISTER

Technique: Alternate eighth note picking should be used throughout.

EDCAG position: Shape 1 G minor pentatonic scale riff mixed with shape 4 power chords.

Harmonic content: Diatonic content from the G minor pentatonic scale with the ♭5 added from the G blues scale.

Guitar settings: Bridge pickup, ideally on a humbucker-equipped guitar.

Amp settings: Select distortion channel to achieve a full, fat, overdriven tone.

Effects: None.

WATCH OUT FOR

THE SLIDE FROM D♭ TO C AT THE END OF THE SECOND BAR. SLIDE WITH YOUR THIRD FINGER, TO LEAVE YOUR FIRST FINGER FREE FOR THE B♭ THAT FOLLOWS.

FILL NO. 1:
VERSE PUNCTUATION

Content wise, there is little difference between a lick and a fill, but their positioning in a song differs. While licks are used to build a guitar solo, fills are commonly played "in the gaps" between vocal phrases. They need to be subtle and concise to avoid treading on the singer's toes. Conversely, if they are boring and uninteresting, they will actually spoil the song, so it's important to get the balance just right. In this example, each fill occurs at the end of a four-bar vocal phrase where the singer would usually be holding a long note. The identical rhythmic phrasing maintains a sense of unity and structure, and avoids upstaging the vocal performance with too much diversity.

Verse punctuation should complement the vocal.

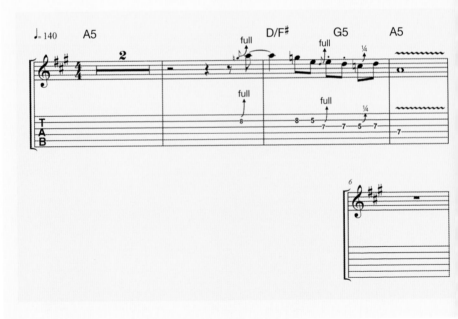

RIFF REGISTER

Technique: Use eighth note alternate picking to keep the phrases rhythmic and fluid.

EDCAG position: Shape 1 A minor pentatonic.

Harmonic content: A minor pentatonic with the minor third (C) bent a quarter tone sharp to hint at the underlying major tonality.

Guitar settings: Bridge pickup with tone rolled off slightly.

Amp settings: Distortion channel with preamp gain set at around three o'clock.

Effects: None.

WATCH OUT FOR

BENDING THE NOTE ACCURATELY
AT THE START OF EACH PHRASE
AND HOLDING IT AT PITCH.

FILL NO. 2:
VERSE INTERLUDE

It's common practice for songs to feature the first two verses
back to back, raising the sense of anticipation by making the
listener "wait" for the first chorus. In this scenario it's often
the guitarist's job to play a fill between the verses, usually no
more than four bars long, as in this example. It's important
to remember to exercise restraint in these circumstances—it's
a musical interlude, not an opportunity to shred! Many
players compose their interlude fills, so the best ones become
inseparable from the song and are repeated note for note in
live performances. This example is built from three phrases:
two short "question and answer"-style phrases, followed by
a longer, two-bar concluding phrase.

Verse interludes should be musical and controlled.

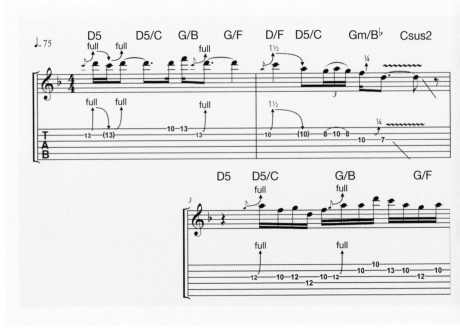

RIFF REGISTER

Technique: Use sixteenth note alternate picking throughout.

EDCAG position: Shape 1 D minor pentatonic.

Harmonic content: D minor pentatonic. Notice that, when playing in a minor key, quarter-tone bends can still be applied to the minor third (F) of the scale.

Guitar settings: Bridge or neck pickup, with volume and tone up full.

Amp settings: Select distortion channel, and set preamp level to seven o'clock.

Effects: Echo pedal set with eighth note repeats and wet/dry mix at 25 percent.

WATCH OUT FOR

KEEPING THOSE POWER CHORD SHAPES INTACT AS YOU SLIDE ALONG THE NECK.

D5   D5/C Gm/B♭ C sus2

FILL NO. 3:
CHORUS PUNCTUATION

Just as fills can be added to verses, they can also be appended to choruses. However, it's more effective to add them during the final chorus, when extra interest and climactic enhancement are required. You'll notice that the fills in this example are quite short and sparse—it's important not to compromise the vocal melody by overplaying. Both fills have near identical rhythmic phrasing (to provide melodic coherence). They also finish promptly at the beginning of the bar (to keep out of the way of the vocals).

Dinner at the diner in the 1950s.

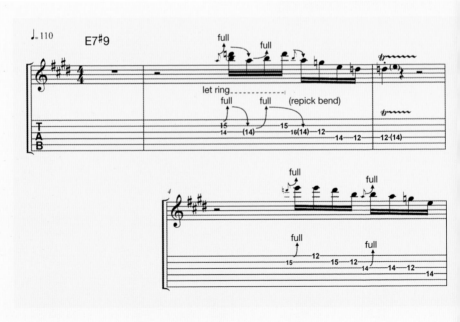

RIFF REGISTER

Technique: Played pickstyle using alternate sixteenth note picking throughout.

EDCAG position: Shape 1 E minor pentatonic scale on the twelfth fret.

Harmonic content: E minor pentatonic scale effectively enhancing color tones of the E7#9 chord.

Guitar settings: Neck position, with tone control on full.

Amp settings: Distortion channel with preamp setting on seven o'clock.

Effects: None.

WATCH OUT FOR

THE OPENING DOUBLE-STOP BEND. USE YOUR FOURTH FINGER TO FRET THE HIGH D ON THE FIFTEENTH FRET AND YOUR REMAINING FINGERS TO BEND THE THIRD STRING (DON'T REPICK THE BEND UNTIL INDICATED TO DO SO).

FILL NO. 4:
ENDING LICK

Adding a fill during the end of a song will enhance the climax. The notes in this fill not only fit the shifting harmonic sequence well, but as the chord sequence rises the fill descends. This pleasing musical effect is known as *contrary motion*. Ending fills are the trickiest to get right. Not only must the fill conclude at a very specific point, but the end is the part of a song that your audience is most likely to remember! You may well have just played a jaw-dropping solo, but mess up the ending and your audience will be unimpressed. For this reason it's best to have a few ending fills like this one "up your sleeve," ready to call into action just when you need them.

Chicago: The hometown of the blues.

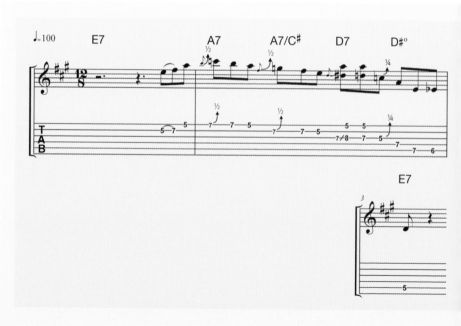

RIFF REGISTER

Technique: Alternate eighth note picking with hybrid picking required for the double stops in the second bar.

EDCAG position: Shape 1 A major pentatonic and A minor blues scale.

Harmonic content: Uses A major pentatonic to outline tonic dominant (A7) and A minor blues scale to outline IV7 and IV°7 (D7 and E♭°7) chords.

Guitar settings: Middle pickup setting (all pickups on) with tone rolled off slightly.

Amp settings: Select distortion channel to achieve a full, fat, overdriven tone.

Effects: None.

WATCH OUT FOR

OVERBENDING THE HALF-STEP BENDS ON THE FIRST AND SECOND BEATS OF BAR 1. CHECK YOUR PITCH BY PLAYING THE FRETTED NOTE FIRST.

B♭7   A7

Jimi Hendrix performs at the
Boston Garden.

10 KILLER CLASSIC ROCK ALBUMS
YOU CAN'T AFFORD TO IGNORE

1 Jimi Hendrix • *Electric Ladyland* (1968)
2 Santana • *Abraxas* (1970)
3 The Who • *Who's Next* (1971)
4 The Rolling Stones • *Sticky Fingers* (1971)
5 Deep Purple • *Made in Japan* (1972)
6 Wishbone Ash • *Argus* (1972)
7 Boston • *Boston* (1976)
8 The Eagles • *Hotel California* (1976)
9 Dire Straits • *Dire Straits* (1978)
10 Foreigner • *4* (1981)

CLASSIC ROCK

The 1960s and 1970s were incredibly fertile, innovative, and progressive decades in the history of popular music. Many of the bands we know and love today didn't arrive on the scene fully formed, and they usually didn't start selling in significant quantities until their third or fourth albums. For instance, The Who released their first album in 1965, but multi-platinum sales would elude them until *Tommy*, their fourth album, was released in 1969. Today's artists are expected to achieve instant sales, so many of the bands we know and love simply wouldn't achieve their full potential in today's music business.

To appreciate the change in society that was also a huge factor in making this musical revolution possible, we need to look to the decade that preceded it. During the 1950s, the UK was enveloped in a blanket of postwar austerity—even rationing continued well into the middle of the decade. By the 1960s, everyone was hungry for change; it was a decade of optimism and the return of the "feel-good factor." Unemployment plummeted,

consumerism rocketed, and people enjoyed leisure time for the first time in history. The UK's film, music, and fashion industry was flourishing, and if you weren't into it you weren't hip!

Music today doesn't have the same social relevance that it once did. Live venues are thin on the ground, primarily because interest in live music has waned. As a result, there are fewer places for bands to cut their teeth, so it's no wonder that there are fewer new acts coming through. Because of this, interest in classic rock is stronger than ever. Teenagers are choosing to listen to the music that their parents, or even grandparents, listened to, which would have been unheard of in previous generations. There's a plethora of radio stations dedicated to playing nothing but classic rock music, and the careers of many bands have been revived by the increase in demand for this most enduring of all rock genres. So grab your guitar and get set for a revealing journey through the techniques, tips, and tricks of rock's greatest pioneers!

RIFF NO. 1:

ROGER McGUINN STYLE

The Byrds' infectious melodies, jangly guitar riffs, and lush vocal harmonies were instrumental in defining the sound of classic rock. Like many bands in the 1960s, their sound quickly evolved and they soon became associated with the psychedelic rock movement. The band's principal guitarist, songwriter, and vocalist, Roger McGuinn is said to have bought a Rickenbacker electric 12-string guitar after seeing the Beatles' movie *A Hard Day's Night*. In this example, the riff is played once on a regular electric and then doubled on a 12-string. If you can't get hold of an electric 12-string, don't worry—it still sounds cool on a six-string!

Roger McGuinn performing in the 1960s.

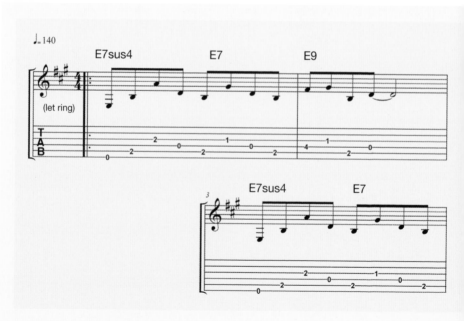

CLASSIC ROCK INTRO RIFFS

RIFF REGISTER

Technique: Use alternate eighth note picking, allowing the notes to ring throughout.

EDCAG position: Open shape 1 E7 chord.

Harmonic content: Intro riff built on the V7 chord in the key of A major. Suspended fourth and ninth sounds are added, creating interest by the use of tension and release.

Guitar settings: Middle pickup setting (both pickups), to create a warm, jangly tone.

Amp settings: Select clean channel; keep preamp settings low and master volume high.

Effects: Tremolo pedal.

WATCH OUT FOR

ACCIDENTALLY MUTING THE OPEN FOURTH STRING BY TOUCHING IT WITH YOUR SECOND FINGER. KEEPING THE FINGER AT 90 DEGREES TO THE FRETBOARD WILL HELP TO AVOID THIS.

N.C.

RIFF NO. 2:

PETE TOWNSHEND STYLE

The Who's incendiary, equipment-smashing performances are the stuff of rock & roll legend. With an exhilarating sound that matched their stage show, the band quickly achieved superstar status. By the early 1970s, the rhythm section's style had been perfected: Pete Townshend's huge "wall of sound" power-chord riffs, Keith Moon's explosive and exciting drumming, and the melodic bass lines provided by John "The Ox" Entwistle. This riff is typical of the band during this period and is great fun to play. Like many rock guitarists today, Pete often double-tracked his rhythm parts in the studio to create his trademark guitar sound. This technique has been reproduced on the track, with two separately recorded guitar parts panned hard left and right creating a big, sonorous sound.

Pete Townshend performing onstage.

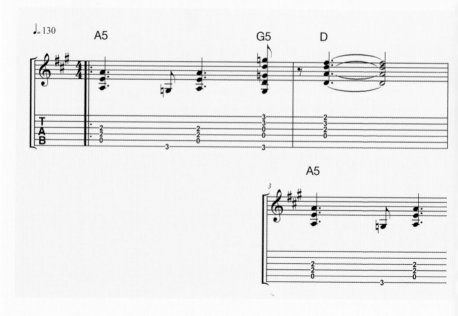

CLASSIC ROCK INTRO RIFFS

RIFF REGISTER

Technique: Use alternate eighth note strumming throughout, "ghosting" your picking hand over the strings when sustaining the long chords.

EDCAG position: Basic open chord shape including the shape 4 A5 and shape 5 G5 power chords.

Harmonic content: Power chords mixed with major chords. The open G5 voicing

creates a huge sound when played with overdrive.

Guitar settings: Bridge pickup, with volume and tone on full.

Amp settings: Select overdrive channel, and set preamp level to six o'clock.

Effects: None.

WATCH OUT FOR

HITTING THE STRINGS WITH AGGRESSION BUT WITHOUT COMPROMISING ON ACCURACY.

RIFF NO. 3:

RITCHIE BLACKMORE STYLE

Ritchie Blackmore was Deep Purple's original guitarist and bandleader. Famed not just for his virtuoso guitar playing but also for his artistic tantrums and frequent sacking of band members, Purple have often been credited as being the pioneers of heavy metal. By today's standards, however, they sit more comfortably at the "heavy" end of the classic rock genre. Blackmore cites country music legend Chet Atkins as one of his early idols. A legacy of the Chet influence is Blackmore's use of hybrid picking when playing riffs. This creates a tighter, more precise sound than using the pick alone and is used to good effect in this Blackmore-esque example.

Ritchie Blackmore performing in 1973.

RIFF REGISTER

Technique: Hybrid picking—pick the lower notes with your pick and the higher notes with your third (*m*) finger.

EDCAG position: Shape 1 G minor pentatonic double stops mixed with open third and fourth strings.

Harmonic content: Diatonic fourths played against a tonic G bass pedal create an exciting riff typical of Blackmore's style.

Guitar settings: Middle pickup position on a Fender Strat.

Amp settings: Select overdrive channel; set preamp level around nine o'clock.

Effects: None.

WATCH OUT FOR

MAKING A MEAL OF FRETTING THE DOUBLE STOPS! USE A SEMI-BARRE ACROSS THE RELEVANT STRINGS USING YOUR FIRST OR THIRD FINGERS.

C5

RIFF NO. 4:
ANDY POWELL STYLE

British rock band Wishbone Ash achieved their legendary status in the early 1970s as one of the first bands to feature harmony twin lead guitar. The rock media has frequently hailed original lead guitarists Andy Powell and Ted Turner as being among the most important and influential rock guitar double acts of the 1970s. This example focuses on Andy Powell's cool riffing style, another of this band's great strengths. Unlike many of his contemporaries, Powell played his riffs with a clean sound, frequently using major triads to create Wishbone Ash's distinctive rock sound. This riff illustrates how effective this triadic approach can be, particularly when they are sounded against the open D string.

Wishbone Ash's *Argus* (1972).

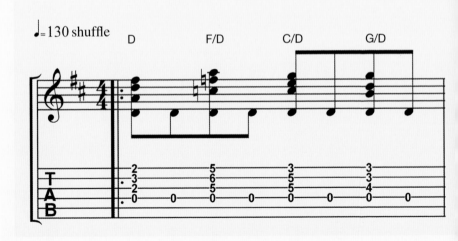

RIFF REGISTER

Technique: Use downpicks throughout to create a strong, rhythmic delivery.

EDCAG position: Shape 2 (D & F), shape 4 (C), and shape 1 (G) major chords.

Harmonic content: Including non-diatonic chords (F and C) prevents this major triad-based riff from sounding too sweet and "inside."

Guitar settings: Bridge pickup, with tone rolled off a little to avoid an over-bright sound.

Amp settings: Select clean channel; set preamp level low and output level high.

Effects: None.

WATCH OUT FOR

MOVING QUICKLY FROM THE OPEN D CHORD TO THE G ON THE FIFTH FRET. AS THIS IS BASED ON THE SAME CHORD SHAPE, KEEP THE SHAPE INTACT AS YOU MOVE YOUR HAND UP THE NECK.

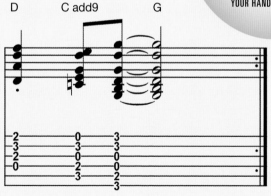

RIFF NO. 1:
MICK JONES STYLE

Ever since the early days of rock & roll, echo has been one of the most consistently used guitar effects. In the 1950s it was generated by tape-based machines, which remained the mainstay of guitar delay until the emergence of digital pedals in the late 1970s. Today compact digital pedals emulate the warm sound of the original tape echo machines, while virtual computer plug-ins are capable of providing multi-layered delays that can swirl around a room in 5.1 (six channel surround sound)! Foreigner's 1981 album *Foreigner 4* is chockablock with killer riffs courtesy of guitarist and principal songwriter Mick Jones. This example illustrates how Mr. Jones used delay to create a hypnotic, driving riff—perfect for the verse of a classic rock-style song.

Mick Jones performing in 1985.

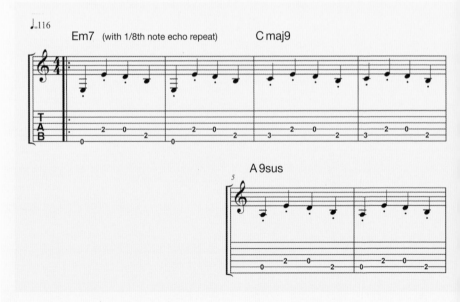

RIFF REGISTER

Technique: Use downpicks throughout, damping the strings with your picking hand to keep them short.

EDCAG position: Open shape 1 E Aeolian (natural minor) scale.

Harmonic content: The repeated upper notes of the riff E, D, and B, are sounded against a shifting root. This implies the chord sequence Em7, Cmaj9, and A9sus.

Guitar settings: Bridge pickup setting, to provide a bright, cutting tone.

Amp settings: Select overdrive channel, setting preamp level to around four o'clock.

Effects: Digital delay set to provide eighth note repeats.

WATCH OUT FOR

KEEPING YOUR TIMING ROCK SOLID—
DON'T FORGET THAT AN OUT-OF-TIME
NOTE WILL BE REPEATED BY THE
DELAY PEDAL!

E m7

RIFF NO. 2:
THE DOOBIE BROTHERS STYLE

Throughout their long career, the Doobie Brothers embraced many styles, from the hard rock of their formative years to the sophisticated jazz and soul infusions of the Michael McDonald era. This example illustrates the funkier side of the band's repertoire while still under the direction of original guitarist and vocalist Tom Johnston during the early 1970s. Many rock guitarists shy away from playing funk because it demands the use of unfamiliar techniques: fast sixteenth note strumming patterns and fretting-hand string damping. It's a technique that's worth practicing, as inventive rock players have been incorporating funky rhythms in their music since the 1960s. As well as paying homage to the classic Doobie Brothers style, this riff illustrates how effective a funk-based comp can sound as a song's verse riff.

The Doobie Brothers in 1979.

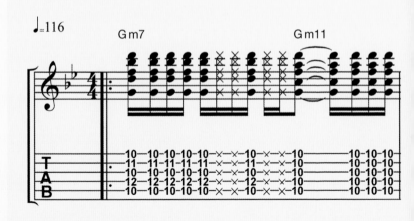

RIFF REGISTER

Technique: Use alternate sixteenth note strumming throughout. To achieve the muted chords, simply release the pressure of your fretting hand without lifting your fingers off the strings.

EDCAG position: Shape 4 Gm7 barre chord.

Harmonic content: Lifting the second and third fingers off the strings creates the ambiguous Gm11 sounds at the end of each bar.

Guitar settings: Position 4 (neck and middle pickups) on a Fender Strat.

Amp settings: Select clean channel, keep preamp level low and output volume high.

Effects: None.

WATCH OUT FOR

KEEPING YOUR PICKING HAND STRUMMING CONTINUOUS—EVEN SIXTEENTH NOTES.

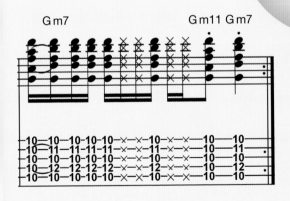

RIFF NO. 3:

TOM SCHOLZ STYLE

Multi-instrumentalist, vocalist, producer, and songwriter
Tom Scholz unsuccessfully peddled his band's demos to
record companies for six long years. Nearly out of money,
his last-ditch attempt was directed at Epic Records. The
label promptly signed the band and the demos became
Boston's eponymously titled first album. Released in 1976, it
remains the second-biggest-selling debut album in American
chart history (only beaten by Guns N' Roses' *Appetite for
Destruction* in 1987). Boston's debut remains a highly
influential album to this day; it set the blueprint that rock
bands would copy for decades. In this verse-style riff, Scholz's
skillful arranging tricks are also revealed. By keeping the riff
clean (it's also doubled on acoustic) and the drums light, the
scene is set for the blockbuster chorus that would follow.

Tom Scholz performing onstage.

WATCH OUT FOR

LETTING ALL THE NOTES RING INTO EACH
OTHER. BE CAREFUL NOT TO ACCIDENTALLY
DAMP THE OPEN STRINGS BY TOUCHING
THEM WITH YOUR FRETTING
FINGERS.

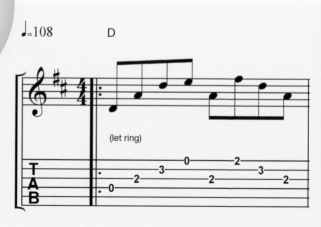

CLASSIC ROCK VERSE RIFFS

RIFF REGISTER

Technique: Can be played in three ways: using alternate picking, using economy picking (i.e., pick the first three notes with a downpick), or fingerstyle.

EDCAG position: Shape 2 (D), shape 3 (Csus2), and shape 5 (G/B) open chords.

Harmonic content: D major picking sequence given a bluesy twist with the inclusion of non-diatonic C root notes in the second bar.

Guitar settings: Bridge pickup setting.

Amp settings: Select clean channel, keep preamp level low and output volume high.

Effects: Chorus pedal.

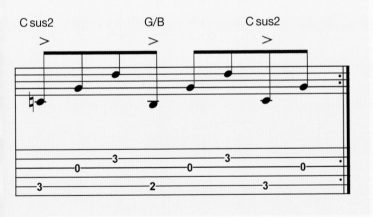

RIFF NO. 4:

JIMI HENDRIX STYLE

The legacy of Jimi Hendrix can still be clearly heard in emerging players today. There was a timeless quality to his fiery, funky, wild, bluesy, and supercool playing that has never been equaled. The chord featured in this riff (E7#9) became known as the "Hendrix chord," because it featured in so many of his famous riffs. Although he didn't invent the chord (it had been used by jazz musicians since the days of bebop), he was one of the first rock musicians to embrace its ambiguous sound. This chord has both the major and minor third (a #9 is the enharmonic equivalent of a 3), making it perfect for Hendrix's "rule-bending" approach to songwriting. This riff features the chord high up on the sixth fret—a favorite location of Hendrix's because he could sound it against the low open E string.

Jimi Hendrix performing onstage.

RIFF REGISTER

Technique: Use sixteenth note alternate picking/strumming throughout. Damped notes/chords should be played by muting the strings with your fretting hand.

EDCAG position: Shape 1 E minor pentatonic riff content mixed with a shape 3/shape 4 E7#9 chord.

Harmonic content: Quarter-tone bends hint at the underlying major tonality, but keep the listener guessing. Further harmonic ambiguity is provided by the final E7#9 chord.

Guitar settings: Neck pickup (ideally) on a Fender Strat.

Amp settings: Select overdrive channel, and set preamp around six o'clock.

Effects: None.

WATCH OUT FOR

PLAYING IT ACCURATELY AND RHYTHMICALLY. HENDRIX WAS A CONSUMMATE RHYTHM PLAYER— ALL OF HIS RIFFS HAVE HIGH LEVELS OF GROOVE!

E 7#9

RIFF NO. 1:
JOE WALSH STYLE

Joe Walsh was already an established solo artist when he joined forces with the Eagles in 1975. This seemingly retrograde career move was in fact a masterstroke—the album that followed in 1976, *Hotel California*, became a multi-million-seller and established Walsh as an international superstar. This example is based on Walsh's work during the period and highlights his tight and funky riffing approach. By the mid-1970s, multi-track recording and big budgets were the norm for bands of the Eagles stature, so guitar parts were multilayered to create a fat, larger-than-life sound. On the CD you can hear that the riff has not only been double-tracked, but also doubled by a third guitar part an octave higher. To play this part, simply start the riff on the 12th fret.

Joe Walsh before a concert in 1975.

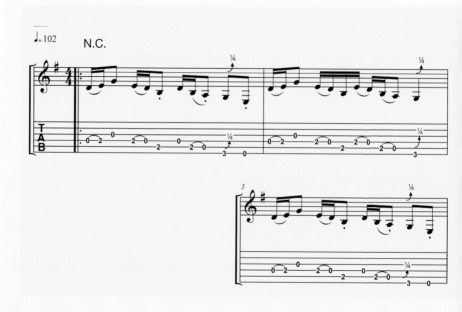

RIFF REGISTER

Technique: Use alternate sixteenth note picking throughout.

EDCAG position: Open shape 1 E minor pentatonic scale.

Harmonic content: Derived from the notes of the E minor pentatonic scale, with no harmonic accompaniment.

Guitar settings: Bridge pickup setting with tone backed off slightly.

Amp settings: Select overdrive channel, setting preamp level to around 8 o'clock.

Effects: None.

WATCH OUT FOR

PLAYING THE SLURS (HAMMER-ONS AND PULL-OFFS) RHYTHMICALLY. IT'S IMPORTANT THAT THE NOTE LENGTHS ARE NOT COMPROMISED BY CARELESS TECHNIQUE.

RIFF NO. 2:
KEITH RICHARDS STYLE

By the late 1960s Keith Richards had adopted the open G tuning (much loved by American bluesmen) because of its full, resonant sound. He also removed the sixth string so that he could play chords by simply barring across the fret with one finger–extensions and inversions could then easily be added with the second and third fingers. It was this distinctive-sounding tuning that Richards used to record the iconic riffs of "Brown Sugar," "Honky Tonk Women," "Start Me Up," and many more. To play in this tuning you don't need to remove your sixth string, but you will need to retune your first string (down a tone to D), your fifth string (down a tone to G), and your sixth string (also down a tone to D).

The Rolling Stones' *Sticky Fingers* (1971).

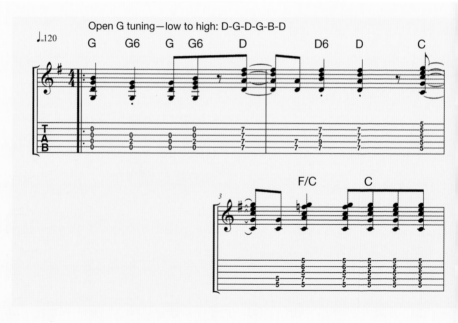

RIFF REGISTER

Technique: Use alternate eighth note strumming throughout to achieve a rhythmic delivery.

EDCAG position: Shape 4 major chords in open G tuning.

Harmonic content: Open tuning allows the classic rock & roll chug riff to be played across four strings instead of just two. It also allows the inclusion of the major third.

Guitar settings: Bridge pickup setting on a Fender Telecaster.

Amp settings: Select overdrive channel, keeping preamp level around two o'clock and master level on full.

Effects: None.

WATCH OUT FOR
CREATING THAT ALL ESSENTIAL LAIDBACK GROOVE—DON'T PUSH THE BEAT.

N.C.

let ring

RIFF NO. 3:
CARLOS SANTANA STYLE

Carlos Santana fused his love of the blues with the Latin American music of his homeland to create an exciting new sound. His legendary performance at Woodstock in 1969 instantly established him and his band, Santana, as worldwide superstars. Carlos frequently incorporates a high level of dynamics in his playing, which has been faithfully reproduced in this example. The opening two-bar riff is played forte (loud) and contrasted with a mezzo-piano (moderately soft) *montuno*-style guitar vamp based on arpeggiated chords. Contrasting volume levels can be created simply by varying your pick attack: pick harder during the single-note riff and softer during the chord vamp. It is worth practicing to develop a dynamic picking technique as it will make your playing sound more musical and professional.

Carlos Santana performing in 1981.

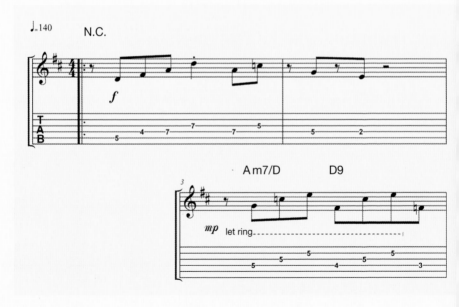

RIFF REGISTER

Technique: Alternate eighth note picking throughout, with controlled picking dynamics.

EDCAG position: Shape 4 arpeggios (D7 and C7) for the riff; shape 3 partial chord voicings (D9 and C9) for the vamp.

Harmonic content: Although there is no chordal accompaniment in the first two bars, the unison arpeggio-based riffs clearly outline the C7 to D7 chord sequence.

Guitar settings: Neck pickup, with volume rolled off slightly to control overdrive.

Amp settings: Select overdrive channel, and set preamp level to five o'clock.

Effects: None.

WATCH OUT FOR

LETTING THE NOTES OF THE MONTUNO VAMP RING INTO EACH OTHER IN THE THIRD BAR; FRET ACROSS THE SECOND AND THIRD STRINGS WITH YOUR THIRD FINGER THROUGHOUT.

C9

RIFF NO. 4:

MARK KNOPFLER STYLE

Mark Knopfler hit the big time with the release of Dire
Straits' self-titled debut album in 1978. With punk rock
and new wave music grabbing the headlines in the UK, this
was not an easy time for a "conventional" rock guitarist to
break onto the scene. However, the quality and integrity of
Knopfler's songwriting, combined with his virtuoso guitar
playing, proved to be a winning combination, and the band
recorded a total of six multi-platinum selling albums before
finally disbanding in 1995. Influenced by country legend
Chet Atkins, Knopfler shunned the traditional pick approach
and preferred to play fingerstyle instead. This undoubtedly
helped him to achieve his very "snappy" and precise sound.
This example illustrates how he would use simple three-
note chord shapes to create an effective, catchy riff.

Mark Knopfler performing in 1979.

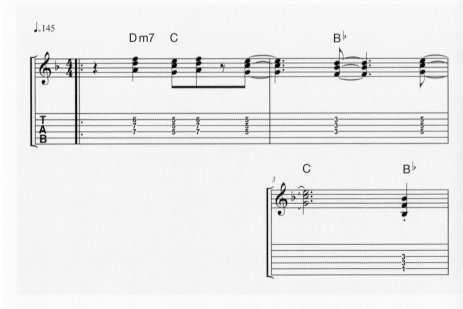

RIFF REGISTER

Technique: Fingerstyle throughout. The three-note chords should be picked simultaneously using your thumb (p), first finger (i), and second finger (m).

EDCAG position: Shape 4 Dm7 chord mixed with shape 4 major triads (C and B).

Harmonic content: Based on a simple minor chord sequence diatonic to the D natural minor scale.

Guitar settings: Position 4 (neck and middle pickups) on a Fender Strat.

Amp settings: Select clean channel, keeping preamp level low and output level high.

Effects: None.

WATCH OUT FOR

KEEPING YOUR FINGERSTYLE TECHNIQUE TIGHT AND RHYTHMIC; PRACTICE THE RIFF AT A SLOWER TEMPO FIRST.

FILL NO. 1:
ANDY POWELL STYLE

The fourth riff in the classic rock intro riffs section provides the perfect backdrop for creating some tasty Andy Powell-style fills. Such a riff as this would typically be reused later in the song. When this happens, the second guitar would take over the riff (in this case, it would have been Wishbone Ash colleague Ted Turner), while the lead guitarist adds short fills in the second bar of each two-bar riff. This is a very effective way to reuse instrumental sections and it's ideal for creating short interludes, i.e., after a chorus or between double verses. In this situation, fills should be kept short—no more than one bar long—with the resolution note falling on the first beat of the following bar.

Andy Powell (left) and Ted Turner (right) performing in 1975.

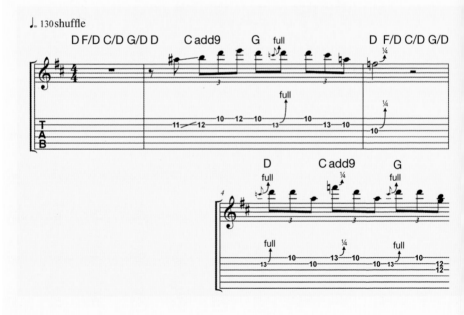

RIFF REGISTER

Technique: Alternate picking where possible (some players prefer to pick down on the first note of every three triplets).

EDCAG position: Shape 1 hybrid major/ minor pentatonic.

Harmonic content: Notes from both the major and minor pentatonic scale have been used to create cool rock & roll flavored fills.

Guitar settings: Bridge pickup setting with tone backed off slightly.

Amp settings: Select overdrive channel, setting preamp level to around five o'clock.

Effects: None.

WATCH OUT FOR

PICKING THE STRINGS CLEANLY AND ACCURATELY (PARTICULARLY IN THE FOURTH BAR) WHEN MOVING QUICKLY FROM STRING TO STRING.

D   F/C C/D G/D

FILL NO. 2:
THE DOOBIE BROTHERS STYLE

In this example we'll be revisiting the Doobie Brothers riff (example 2 of *Classic rock verse riffs*) to illustrate how to add fills to a verse section effectively. It's important not to tread on the singer's toes when you're doing this (or you could find yourself out of a gig). That's why none of the licks in this example start on the first beat of the bar. You'll also notice how consistent the phrasing is—each lick starts on the third beat. Fills like this would be improvised, but this can't be done effectively without experience. Practice this technique by playing along to a metronome or drum loop. Be aware of the beat you're starting each phrase on; it's important to keep focused on your phrasing, so you don't lapse into "noodling" mode!

The Doobie Brothers rehearsing in 1979.

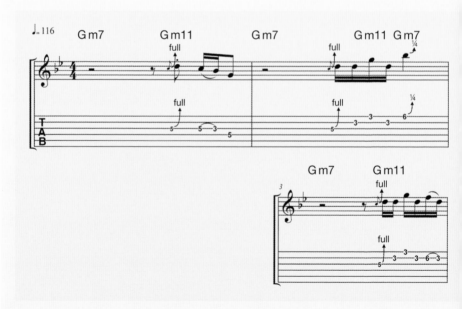

RIFF REGISTER

Technique: Alternate sixteenth note picking with tone and quarter-tone bending.

EDCAG position: Shape 1 and shape 2 G minor pentatonic.

Harmonic content: Tonic minor pentatonic with quarter-tone bend on minor third.

Guitar settings: Middle pickup setting (neck and bridge pickups).

Amp settings: Select overdrive channel and set preamp level to around seven o'clock.

Effects: None.

WATCH OUT FOR

RUSHING THE PHRASES—BE CAREFUL NOT TO "PUSH" PHRASES STARTING ON THE THIRD BEAT.

FILL NO. 3:
MICK TAYLOR STYLE

Mick Taylor joined the Rolling Stones in 1969, shortly
after the departure of Brian Jones. Taylor was a
consummate blues guitarist—he had previously been a
member of John Mayall's Bluesbreakers, following in the
footsteps of Eric Clapton and Peter Green. Taylor was
with the Stones in the period many aficionados regard
as their finest years: 1969 to 1974. This example mimics
Taylor's lyrical style, highlighting his expert ability to
add chorus fills over Keith Richards' powerful rhythm
work. It's important to ensure that your note choices fit
the underlying harmony in this scenario. Notice how the
opening lick resolves on an A note in the second bar in
order to fit the chord change to D that follows.

Mick Taylor performing in 1969.

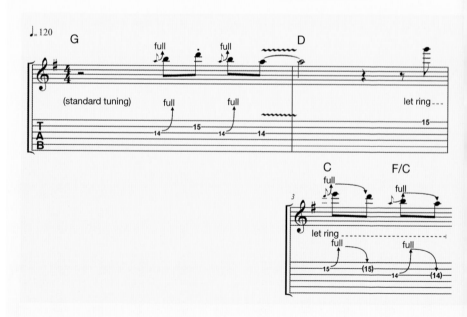

CLASSIC ROCK FILLS

RIFF REGISTER

Technique: Alternate eighth note picking with double-stop bends.

EDCAG position: Shape 5 G major pentatonic.

Harmonic content: Entirely diatonic to the key of G major; resolves on fifth (A) of D in bar 2 and fifth (G) of C in bar 4.

Guitar settings: Bridge pickup with volume rolled off slightly, to control overdrive.

Amp settings: Select overdrive channel, setting preamp level to six o'clock.

Effects: None.

WATCH OUT FOR

ALLOWING THE NOTES TO RING INTO EACH OTHER IN THE THIRD BAR, AS THIS CREATES A COOL, PSEUDO-PEDAL-STEEL EFFECT.

C

FILL NO. 4:
MARK KNOPFLER STYLE

Mark Knopfler is the perfect guitarist to study when you're learning how to effectively add fills to a song, as he's a lead vocalist and a lead guitarist. His fills naturally fall in the gaps between vocal lines, because he has to sing them! In this example, the phrasing is less regimented than in the previous examples. This is because, if you know when you're going to sing, you can be a lot freer with their location. Notice how a "pickup" phrase occurs before the first bar, effectively "framing" the vocal phrase. In the penultimate bar, a rhythmic sixteenth note lick falls under the last note of the melody and concludes under the start of the next vocal phrase.

Mark Knopfler performing onstage.

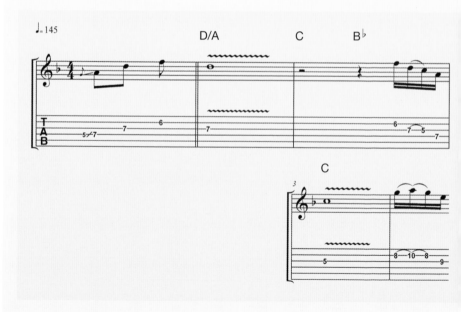

RIFF REGISTER

Technique: For an authentic tone and delivery, fingerstyle technique should be used throughout.

EDCAG position: Shape 4 (bars 1–3) and shape 5 (bar 4) D minor pentatonic.

Harmonic content: With careful note choices, the D minor pentatonic can provide the "inside" notes of the C chord in the fifth bar.

Guitar settings: Position 4 (neck and middle pickups) on a Fender Strat.

Amp settings: Select clean channel, keeping preamp level low and output level high.

Effects: None.

WATCH OUT FOR

PLAYING THE SLURS (HAMMER-ONS AND PULL-OFFS) IN BAR 4 IN TIME. FIRST, PRACTICE WITHOUT SLURRING AT A SLOWER TEMPO.

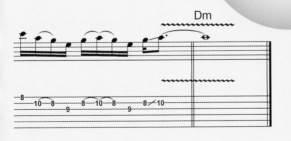

Randy Rhoads, touring with Ozzy Osbourne, during rehearsal in Kansas City in January 1982.

10 KILLER HEAVY METAL ALBUMS YOU CAN'T AFFORD TO IGNORE

1 Black Sabbath • *Paranoid* (1970)
2 Led Zeppelin • *Led Zeppelin IV* (1971)
3 Rainbow • *Rising* (1976)
4 Van Halen • *Van Halen* (1978)
5 Ozzy Osbourne • *Blizzard of Ozz* (1980)
6 Iron Maiden • *The Number of the Beast* (1982)
7 Judas Priest • *Screaming for Vengeance* (1982)
8 Metallica • *Master of Puppets* (1986)
9 Guns N' Roses • *Appetite for Destruction* (1987)
10 Megadeth • *Rust in Peace* (1990)

HEAVY METAL

The term "heavy metal" was first heard in the lyric of Steppenwolf's 1968 single "Born to be Wild," although William Burroughs coined the phrase in his novel *Soft Machine* (1961). Exactly who first used the term "heavy metal" to describe rock music remains hotly disputed to this day. Certainly the early pioneers of the genre—like Black Sabbath, Led Zeppelin, Deep Purple—didn't set out to create it; they just wanted to make the best music they could.

This section deals with the evolution of heavy metal in the late 1960s, the new wave of British heavy metal in the late 1970s, through to the technically proficient American acts of the 1980s. Although some excellent metal bands have emerged since the 1980s, there have been no notable pioneers. From a musician's point of view, the essential techniques of heavy metal guitar were all established by the end of this decade. During the heyday of rock in the 1970s, musicians were allowed greater artistic freedom by the record companies. They were also creating something new that hadn't yet been categorized and pigeonholed by the critics. That's why it's so hard to define a band like Led Zeppelin in modern terms; they recorded in too many different styles (blues, country, reggae, progressive rock, etc.). Paradoxically, along with Black Sabbath, they are widely regarded as one of heavy metal's most important pioneers.

So if you're an aspiring metal guitarist, try thinking of yourself as an aspiring guitarist instead—your playing will be richer for it. From a musician's point of view, whatever style you play, you can't ignore all the wonderful and incredible music out there, from classical to jazz and beyond. And, in the age of the internet, it's easier than ever to listen to whatever you want to, just as long as you know what category it will be filed under at the iTunes store …

RIFF NO. 1:
TONY IOMMI STYLE

There's no better place to start our exploration of all things metal than with the Godfather of heavy metal, Tony Iommi! As guitarist with Black Sabbath, Iommi established all of the crucial heavy metal techniques: power-chord riffing, heavy use of the tritone interval, drop tuning, and double-tracked riffs and solos. The tritone (so called because the interval spans three tones) features in many famous Black Sabbath riffs, and in this example, it is the main focus of the riff. The tritone is a very dissonant interval: during the Middle Ages, its use was outlawed because it was feared it could summon the Devil. No wonder heavy metal guitarists have been using it enthusiastically for decades!

Black Sabbath in 1975.

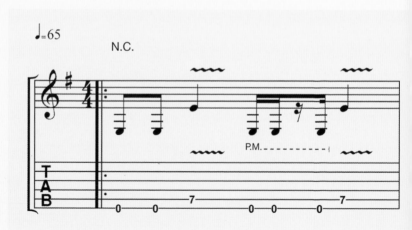

HEAVY METAL INTRO RIFFS

RIFF REGISTER

Technique: Alternate sixteenth note picking and palm muting contrasted with sustained notes and power chords.

EDCAG position: Shape 3 minor blues scale.

Harmonic content: The dissonant, dark quality of the tritone (B♭) is emphasized by sounding it directly after the tonic (E) note.

Guitar settings: Bridge pickup setting with tone and volume on full.

Amp settings: Select distortion channel, setting preamp level high but without "over-saturating" tone.

Effects: None.

WATCH OUT FOR

APPLYING PALM MUTING ONLY WHERE INDICATED; OVERUSE WILL THIN THE IMPACT OF THE RIFF.

B♭5   A5   G5

RIFF NO. 2:
KIRK HAMMETT STYLE

Metallica are one of the most important and significant of the 1980s American heavy metal bands. Kirk Hammett joined the group before the band recorded their first album, *Kill 'Em All*, in 1983. His riffs set new standards in the world of metal and he is famed for his use of constant downpicking, even at blazing tempos. Hammett also made good use of palm muting, a technique that was used to create the menacing and rhythmically intense riffs that became Metallica's trademark. This example illustrates how Hammett likes to base his riffs on the sixth string, alternating single notes and power chords against the open string. At this tempo you will probably find consecutive downpicking too demanding. If so, use conventional alternate eighth note picking.

Kirk Hammett performing in 1986.

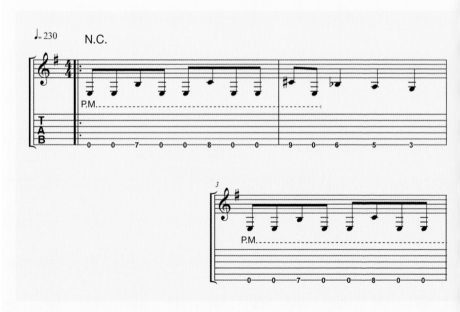

RIFF REGISTER

Technique: Strict downpicking throughout.

EDCAG position: Chromatic riff played along the sixth string based on shapes 2, 3, and 4 of the E Aeolian/Dorian modes.

Harmonic content: E minor riff that uses both the major and minor sixth interval (C and C#) along with the tritone (B♭) to create varying degrees of dissonance.

Guitar settings: Bridge pickup with volume and tone on full.

Amp settings: Select distortion channel and set preamp level to full.

Effects: None.

WATCH OUT FOR

PLAYING STRICTLY IN TIME, BUILD TEMPO SLOWLY TO BUILD YOUR TECHNIQUE AND CONTROL.

RIFF NO. 3:

EDDIE VAN HALEN STYLE

Eddie Van Halen literally rocked the guitar world when his band Van Halen exploded onto the music scene with their debut album *Van Halen* in 1978. His pyrotechnical tapping technique and virtuoso solos changed the way heavy metal guitar would be played forever. While much has been made of Eddie's incredible soloing skills, his riffing style is frequently overlooked. Like all of the great players, he knows exactly how important the humble riff is—it can make or break a good song. In this example, you can hear some heavy flanging. This was another of Eddie's trademarks: he frequently stomped on his MXR (M117) flanger pedal "mid-riff" to create dramatic, vocal-like, vowel sounds.

Eddie Van Halen performing in 1984.

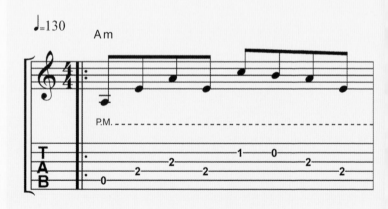

HEAVY METAL INTRO RIFFS

RIFF REGISTER

Technique: Alternate eighth note picking with heavy palm muting.

EDCAG position: Shape 1 open Am chord and shape 5 open G7 chord.

Harmonic content: Diatonic A minor riff based on arpeggiated open chords.

Guitar settings: Bridge pickup with volume rolled off to control overdrive.

Amp settings: Select distortion channel, and set preamp level to seven o'clock.

Effects: Flanger.

WATCH OUT FOR

KEEPING YOUR PICKING RHYTHM EVEN
AND CONSISTENT WHILE APPLYING
PALM MUTING.

G 7

RIFF NO. 4:
IRON MAIDEN STYLE

Iron Maiden's career was launched on the crest of the new wave of British heavy metal in the mid-1970s. As the new ambassadors of heavy metal, their distinctive style would prove to be just as enduring and popular as that of any of the original metal bands. The band's twin-guitar lineup has featured many players over the years. The most important and influential of these were Dave Murray and Adrian Smith, who were members throughout the 1980s, when the group recorded their most critically acclaimed albums. Their live performances remain as exhilarating and exciting as ever, while their 2010 album *The Final Frontier* hit the number one spot in nine countries simultaneously.

Iron Maiden's *The Number of the Beast* (1982).

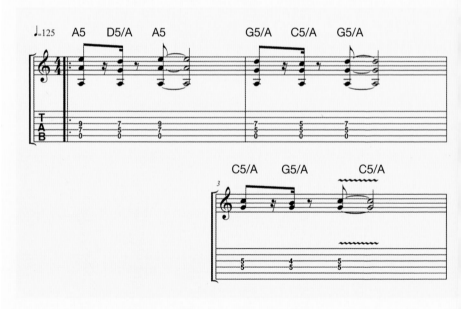

HEAVY METAL INTRO RIFFS

RIFF REGISTER

Technique: Use downpicks throughout to create an even, consistent performance.

EDCAG position: Shape 2, shape 4, and shape 5 power chords.

Harmonic content: Three-note and two-note diatonic (to A minor) power chords sounded against a tonic pedal bass note.

Guitar settings: Bridge pickup with volume rolled off slightly to control distortion.

Amp settings: Select distortion channel, and set preamp level high (around eight or nine o'clock).

Effects: None.

WATCH OUT FOR

PLAYING THE SYNCOPATED SIXTEENTH NOTE RHYTHMS ACCURATELY WHEN USING DOWNPICKS EXCLUSIVELY.

G5   A5

RIFF NO. 1:
SLASH STYLE

Rising from the ashes of the 1980s hair metal movement, Guns N' Roses exploded onto the rock scene with their debut album, *Appetite for Destruction*, in 1987. The jury is still out on whether G N' R are heavy metal or hard rock, mainly because of the huge success of their more commercial songs like "Sweet Child o' Mine," "Patience," and "Knockin' on Heaven's Door." The first album was probably their best and contains some of Slash's coolest and heaviest guitar work. This example illustrates Slash's distinctive style during the early G N' R period. In many ways it's closer to the style of the original metal bands such as Sabbath and Zeppelin, where the drums often pinned down sixteenth note guitar riffs with a slow half-time groove.

Slash performing in 1987.

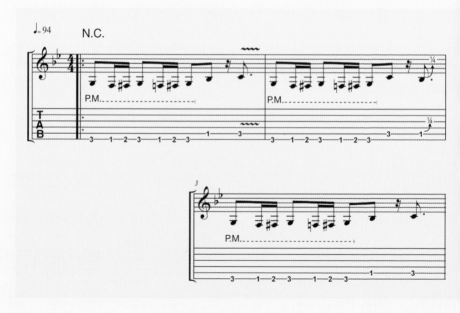

HEAVY METAL VERSE RIFFS

RIFF REGISTER

Technique: Alternate sixteenth note picking with heavy palm muting.

EDCAG position: Shape 1 G minor blues scale.

Harmonic content: Old-school, single note riff with the solitary power chord stated on IV (C5).

Guitar settings: Bridge pickup setting with tone and volume on full.

Amp settings: Select distortion channel, setting preamp level high.

Effects: None.

WATCH OUT FOR

ACCURATELY INTERPRETING THE HEAVILY SYNCOPATED SIXTEENTH NOTE GROOVE. USE "GHOSTED" DOWNPICKS ON THE SIXTEENTH RESTS.

RIFF NO. 2:

JIMMY PAGE STYLE

Some people argue vociferously that Led Zeppelin were absolutely not heavy metal. This is true, but there's no doubt you could pick a Zeppelin track to fit into *every* chapter in this book. They defied categorization, and that's why they were so good. By modern standards, they may not sound particularly heavy, but they were true pioneers of the genre. This was in part due to the incredibly powerful drumming of John Bonham, and part Jimmy Page's talent for writing heavy, bluesy riffs and his pioneering studio production techniques. This riff is inspired by Jimmy Page's work during the band's early career—a period that many agree is their heaviest and best.

Led Zeppelin performing in 1975.

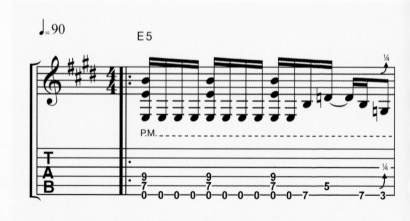

RIFF REGISTER

Technique: Alternate sixteenth note picking with gentle palm muting applied throughout.

EDCAG position: Using a shape 4 E5 power chord but using mainly shape 3 of the E minor pentatonic scale for the riff.

Harmonic content: Steeped in the blues tradition, Page was a master of harmonic ambiguity, so, while this riff is in the key of

E major, the major third would not be stated until the song's chorus.

Guitar settings: Bridge pickup with volume and tone on full.

Amp settings: Select distortion channel and set preamp level to around seven o'clock.

Effects: None.

WATCH OUT FOR

KEEPING THE CONSTANT SIXTEENTH NOTE
RIFF SOUNDING RELAXED AND
"IN THE POCKET."

RIFF NO. 3:
MEGADETH STYLE

During the 1990s the original Megadeth members, Dave Mustaine (lead vocals and guitar) and Dave Ellefson (bass guitar and backing vocals), were augmented by newcomers Marty Friedman on lead guitar and Nick Menza on drums. Mustaine and Friedman's machine-gun riffs, which frequently alternated between unison and harmony, were doubled by Ellefson's bass and Menza's lightning-fast double bass drum technique; this defined the "classic" Megadeth signature sound. This example avoids any harmony parts, but you can add them by playing the last two notes in bars 1, 2, and 3 on the fifth string (this works either on the same fret or a fret lower, depending on whether you want to generate perfect fourths or major thirds above).

Megadeth's *Rust in Peace* (1990).

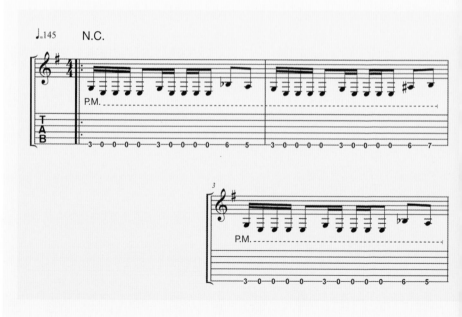

RIFF REGISTER

Technique: Fast, alternate sixteenth note picking, with light palm muting.

EDCAG position: Riff focuses on shape 2 of the E minor blues scale. Power chords are shape 2, two note.

Harmonic content: Diatonic E minor blues-scale riff. Some of the lower notes would be harmonized a third higher by a second guitar, creating non-diatonic tensions.

Guitar settings: Bridge pickup with volume and tone on full.

Amp settings: Select distortion channel, and set preamp level to nine o'clock.

Effects: None.

WATCH OUT FOR

IT'S IMPORTANT TO KEEP YOUR SIXTEENTH NOTE PICKING VERY EVEN AND CONSISTENT THROUGHOUT—YOU MAY NEED TO PRACTICE THIS BY BUILDING TEMPO GRADUALLY.

F#5   F5

RIFF NO. 4:
RANDY RHOADS STYLE

When Ozzy Osbourne was fired from Black Sabbath in 1979 (primarily due to his excessive lifestyle), he chose the talented young American guitarist Randy Rhoads as a partner for his solo career. Rhoads was a brilliant musician and a devoted student of classical guitar. His promising career was tragically cut short by a plane crash while on tour in 1982. Although he recorded just two albums with Ozzy, many contemporary rock guitarists have cited Rhoads as a major influence. By mixing rock and classical influences, he achieved a highly individual style, and, after Ritchie Blackmore, was undoubtedly the most important influence on the emerging neoclassical metal genre.

Ozzy Osbourne's *Blizzard of Ozz* (1980).

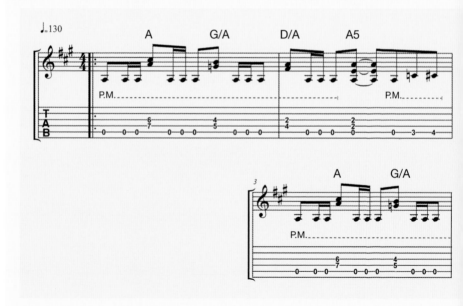

RIFF REGISTER

Technique: Sixteenth note alternate picking combined with palm muting (on lower notes) throughout. Fast three-notes-per-string pull-offs conclude the four-bar sequence.

EDCAG position: Shape 1 and 3 double stops with shape 4 A5 power chord.

Harmonic content: The inclusion of the G natural (in the G/A chord and the fast triplet run) adds harmonic interest to this otherwise diatonic major riff.

Guitar settings: Bridge pickup with volume rolled off slightly to control distortion.

Amp settings: Select distortion channel, setting preamp level at eight o'clock.

Effects: Chorus pedal.

WATCH OUT FOR

THAT FAST TRIPLET RUN! RELEASE YOUR FINGERS WITH A SLIGHT SIDEWAYS "FLICKING" MOTION TO GENERATE CLEAR PULL-OFF NOTES.

D/A   A5

RIFF NO. 1:
MÖTLEY CRÜE STYLE

Black Sabbath's Tony Iommi was the first heavy metal
guitarist to experiment with dropped tunings, which
involves slackening the tuners so the guitar is tuned a
tone (or more) lower than normal. It creates a deeper,
more menacing sound and makes it easier to play faster.
As pioneers of the American "glam metal" movement in
the early 1980s, Mötley Crüe's catchy anthems had pop
sensibility. They were also—for the time—seriously heavy.
This was mainly due to the drop-tuned riffs of lead guitarist
Vince Neil. This example uses drop D tuning—one of the
easiest and quickest ways to get into cool altered tunings.
This tuning allows you to play power chords by simply
barring across the strings with one finger: perfect for
creating fast, low power-chord riffs.

Vince Neil of Mötley Crüe.

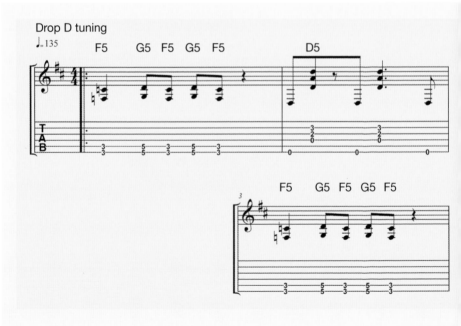

HEAVY METAL CHORUS RIFFS

RIFF REGISTER

Technique: Can be played with alternate eighth note picking or consecutive downpicks for a more powerful sound.

EDCAG position: Shape 1 power chords (drop D barre style).

Harmonic content: Harmonically ambiguous riff that avoids the major third (F#) of the key.

Guitar settings: Bridge pickup setting with tone and volume on full.

Amp settings: Select distortion channel, setting preamp level high.

Effects: None.

WATCH OUT FOR

DAMPING THE UNWANTED HIGHER STRINGS WHEN PLAYING THE POWER CHORDS. TO ACHIEVE THIS, ANGLE YOUR FINGER AWAY FROM THE FRETBOARD AT THE FIRST KNUCKLE.

F5   E5   D5

let ring

RIFF NO. 2:
MOTÖRHEAD STYLE

Motörhead's unique style was achieved by fusing heavy metal with punk rock, a winning formula that has seen the release of an incredible 20 studio albums to date. The most successful of these remains their fourth studio album, *Ace of Spades* (1980). During this period, the band was a classic power-trio lineup with "Fast" Eddie Clarke on guitar. Clarke tuned a half-step lower than concert pitch to achieve a darker, bigger guitar sound. This example reflects the band's unique style during this period—no one else had ever played at this tempo with so much volume before! To save you the hassle of retuning, the example has been recorded in concert pitch.

Motörhead's *Ace of Spades* (1980).

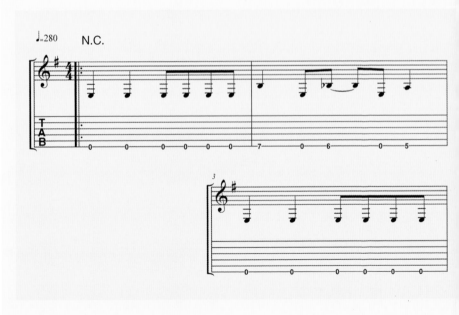

RIFF REGISTER

Technique: Alternate eighth note picking at very fast tempo.

EDCAG position: Riff is based around shape 2 and shape 3 of the E minor blues scale.

Harmonic content: Pure and simple rock & roll riff, consisting of notes from the blues scale.

Guitar settings: Select bridge pickup with volume and tone on full.

Amp settings: Select distortion channel and set preamp level to eight o'clock.

Effects: None.

WATCH OUT FOR

KEEPING YOUR PICKING HAND CONSISTENT AT THIS TEMPO. ALWAYS BUILD TEMPO GRADUALLY OVER MANY PRACTICE SESSIONS.

RIFF NO. 3:
JUDAS PRIEST STYLE

To date, Judas Priest's incredible back catalog comprises no less than 26 albums (including live albums and official compilations). The multi-platinum-selling album *Screaming for Vengeance* (1982) is widely regarded as their best release. Since 1974, Judas Priest's twin lead-guitar lineup has famously featured Glenn Tipton and K. K. Downing; however, Downing announced his retirement from the band in 2011. When playing riffs, Tipton and Downing frequently doubled the same part. This created the tight, rhythmic wall of guitar sound that became Judas Priest's trademark. This example has been double-tracked, to replicate the effect of the two guitarists playing in unison.

Judas Priest in the 1980s.

RIFF REGISTER

Technique: Consecutive downpicking, with palm muting applied on sixth string only.

EDCAG position: Shape 1 F# minor blues scale.

Harmonic content: Diatonic perfect fourths (with the exception of the G in the fourth bar), from F# minor blues scale played against a tonic bass pedal.

Guitar settings: Bridge pickup with tone backed off slightly to warm up the sound.

Amp settings: Select distortion channel, and set preamp level to eight o'clock.

Effects: Chorus pedal.

WATCH OUT FOR

PLAYING THE FOURTHS QUICKLY AND CLEANLY. TRY THE LOWER DOUBLE STOPS ON THE FOURTH AND FIFTH STRINGS WITH YOUR FOURTH AND THIRD FINGER RESPECTIVELY.

E5

RIFF NO. 4:
RAINBOW STYLE

After sacking most of Deep Purple's founder members, Ritchie Blackmore finally quit the band in 1975. He formed Rainbow in the same year. The original lineup featured the late Ronnie James Dio, an outstanding and highly regarded heavy metal vocalist. After the release of the band's debut, Blackmore promptly fired the whole band, with the exception of Dio. Their eagerly anticipated second album, *Rising* (1976), didn't sell in the same numbers as their later, more commercial releases, but it remained their most critically acclaimed album—and certainly one of their most influential. In this example, a "less is more" approach has been used to create a typical Rainbow-style riff that effortlessly locks into the driving shuffle groove.

Rainbow's *Rising* (1976).

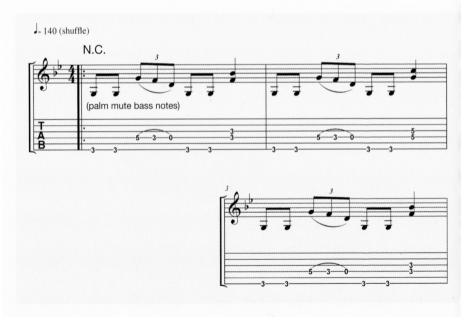

RIFF REGISTER

Technique: Alternate eighth note picking with two-note consecutive pull-offs.

EDCAG position: Shape 1 G minor pentatonic.

Harmonic content: Entirely diatonic to G minor pentatonic. Double stops imply Gm7 and C/G chords over the bass pedal in bars 1 and 2.

Guitar settings: Bridge pickup with volume and tone on full.

Amp settings: Select distortion channel; set preamp level midway and master level high.

Effects: None.

WATCH OUT FOR

DON'T RUSH THE RECURRING TRIPLET PULL-OFF. TO GENERATE CLEAR NOTES, RELEASE YOUR FINGERS WITH A SLIGHT SIDEWAYS "FLICKING" MOTION.

FILL NO. 1:
KIRK HAMMETT STYLE

Kirk Hammett, one of the early masters of shred, "upped the game" for metal players when Metallica released their first album, *Kill 'Em All* in 1983. What set him apart from those that had gone before was his machine-gun-style alternate picking. Many metal players use "tricks" like legato, sweep-picking, and tapping to create fast passages—but Hammett simply picked twice as fast! He is also well-known for adding wah-wah to his fills; however, this effect has been omitted so you can concentrate on your picking and fretting hand coordination. Normally triplet phrases can be picked in a variety of down/up/down permutations, but since the fill is played at breakneck tempo the only option is to use alternate picking. This means you'll be starting the second group of triplets on an up-pick, as indicated in the TAB.

Kirk Hammett onstage in 2009.

WATCH OUT FOR

TRYING TO GET UP TO SPEED TOO SOON. BUILDING YOUR TECHNIQUE TO THIS LEVEL CAN TAKE MONTHS, SO BE PATIENT AND DON'T OVERPRACTICE ONE IDEA (THIS CAN LEAD TO RSI).

HEAVY METAL FILLS

RIFF REGISTER

Technique: Fast, alternate eighth note triplet picking.

EDCAG position: Shapes 3, 4, 5, and 1 of the E Aeolian mode (natural minor).

Harmonic content: All notes are diatonic to the E Aeolian mode.

Guitar settings: Neck pickup setting with tone rolled off halfway.

Amp settings: Select distortion channel, setting preamp level high.

Effects: None.

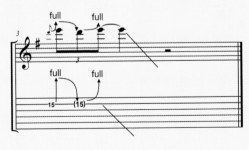

FILL NO. 2:
MICK MARS STYLE

Mötley Crüe's guitarist Mick Mars, like his 1980s contemporaries, fully embraced the techniques of the era. In the first bar of this example, the underlying riff implies the chord of G7, so the fill starts with a tritone double stop that contains the major third (B) and minor seventh (F) of a G7 chord. Tritones are perfect for describing dominant seventh chords, but take a little time to figure out because the root note is not present. In the second bar, the riff returns to the tonic D5 power chord, so the fill reflects this with a legato phrase using the D minor pentatonic scale. Getting your fills to fit a changing chord sequence is tricky. Start by focusing on chord tones—this is much easier than trying to wrestle with a bewildering selection of scale shapes.

Mick Mars performing in 1984.

RIFF REGISTER

Technique: Legato phrasing achieved by consecutive HO/PO/PO slurs (see page 16).

EDCAG position: Shape 3 G7 double-stop voicing, shape 4 D minor pentatonic lick.

Harmonic content: Fill closely follows the IV (G7) to I (D7) harmony of the underlying sequence.

Guitar settings: Bridge pickup with tone and volume controls set high.

Amp settings: Select distortion channel and set preamp level to eight o'clock.

Effects: Chorus pedal.

WATCH OUT FOR

PLAYING THE CONSECUTIVE HO/PO/PO RHYTHMICALLY. BEFORE YOU ADD THE SLURS, PRACTICE THE PHRASE WITH EVERY NOTE PICKED.

D5

FILL NO. 3:

RITCHIE BLACKMORE STYLE

Ritchie Blackmore's influence on not just heavy metal, but on rock music as a whole, has been immense. His soloing style is precise and rhythmic, with frequent use of the whammy bar to add dive bombs (that usually returned to pitch, as in this example) and wild vibrato effects. This fill illustrates the bluesier side of Blackmore's style and contains only notes from the G minor pentatonic scale. It involves three swift position jumps, each new position starting with a tone bend on the second string, so it's quite a tricky lick to play. The final G note is bent down a perfect fourth to D using the whammy bar (it's a good idea to play this note first), which is then released to return the note to pitch. As always, start slowly and build tempo over several practice sessions.

Ritchie Blackmore performing onstage.

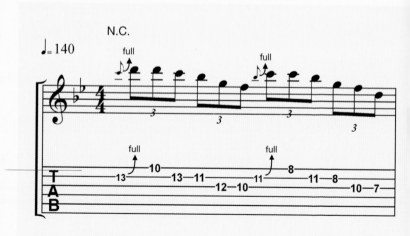

RIFF REGISTER

Technique: Alternate eighth note triplet picking with tone bends.

EDCAG position: Shapes 4, 3, and 1 of the G minor pentatonic scale.

Harmonic content: All fill note diatonic to G minor pentatonic.

Guitar settings: Neck pickup with tone backed off halfway.

Amp settings: Select distortion channel, and set preamp level to seven o'clock.

Effects: None.

WATCH OUT FOR

THE TRICKY POSITION JUMPS EVERY TWO BEATS. THE LAST NOTE IN EACH POSITION SHOULD BE PLAYED WITH YOUR FIRST FINGER, LEAVING YOUR THIRD FINGER FREE TO PLAY THE NEXT BEND.

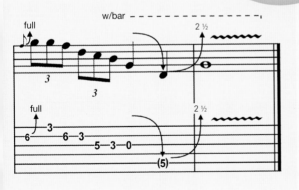

FILL NO. 4:

RANDY RHOADS STYLE

Virtuoso guitarist Randy Rhoads was one of the few "new wave" heavy metal guitarists who were fluent in all of the newly discovered pyrotechnic metal techniques. In his short career, he not only achieved megastar status but also significantly influenced the evolution of the genre. In this example, his proficient two-handed tapping technique is illustrated. This lick is quite tricky to play: not only is it played very fast, but it also involves superimposing sixteenth note sextuplets over the straight sixteenth note groove. Use the first finger of your picking hand to tap the highest note (indicated by the "T" in the TAB). You should keep the first finger of your fretting hand in position on the 10th fret throughout, using your third finger to add the hammer-ons and pull-offs (HO and PO), as indicated in the TAB.

Randy Rhoads performing in 1981.

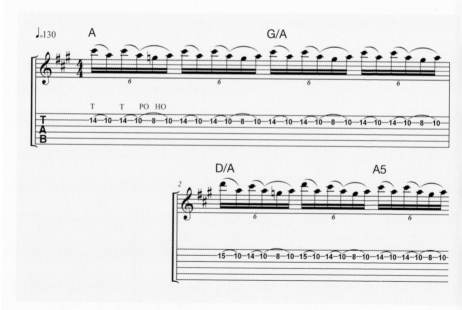

RIFF REGISTER

Technique: Fast two-hand tapping technique.

EDCAG position: Tapped notes are from position 4 of A Mixolydian; lower notes are from shape 2.

Harmonic content: Although the key signature denotes the key of A major, the riff and fill are diatonic to the A Mixolydian dominant mode.

Guitar settings: Bridge pickup with volume and tone on full.

Amp settings: Select distortion channel, and set preamp level on full.

Effects: Chorus pedal.

WATCH OUT FOR

TAKING YOUR TIME TO BUILD TEMPO. SPEND TIME PRACTICING THIS SLOWLY WITH A METRONOME, MAKING SURE THAT THE SEXTUPLETS ARE PLAYED WITH THE CORRECT PHRASING.

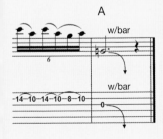

Ian Anderson sings during a performance by Jethro Tull in the 1970s.

10 KILLER PROGRESSIVE ROCK ALBUMS YOU CAN'T AFFORD TO IGNORE

1 The Moody Blues • *Days of Future Passed* (1967)
2 King Crimson • *In the Court of the Crimson King* (1969)
3 Yes • *The Yes Album* (1971)
4 Yes • *Close to the Edge* (1972)
5 Pink Floyd • *The Dark Side of the Moon* (1973)*
6 King Crimson • *Larks' Tongues in Aspic* (1973)
7 Mike Oldfield • *Tubular Bells* (1973)
8 Genesis • *Selling England by the Pound* (1973)
9 Emerson, Lake & Palmer • *Brain Salad Surgery* (1973)
10 Rush • *Permanent Waves* (1980)

* The 1973 albums have been listed in order of release date.

PROGRESSIVE ROCK

Progressive rock—or "prog rock," as it has come to be known—is a genre that's guaranteed to provoke strong opinions. People either love it or hate it. Originally a British phenomenon, it was much loved by the UK's student population (the fanbase was also predominantly male). After enjoying a brief heyday in the early to mid-1970s, its popularity waned and prog spent long years in the wilderness, unloved and unlistened-to except by die-hard fans. However, a resurgence of interest in the genre occurred in the late 1980s and early 1990s with the emergence of derivative bands such as Dream Theater, Phish, Spock's Beard, and Opeth. None of these bands, interestingly, have been from the UK—the new wave of prog emerged from the US and Europe. It's as if the UK is still embarrassed by the "monster" it created and likes to pretend it never happened! This is a great shame, because the prog pioneers really did push the boundaries of rock and created some truly unusual and beautiful music in the process.

In the late 1970s, when the UK was experiencing high unemployment, the general flamboyance and lavish stage sets of the prog bands was criticized for being "out of step" with the youth of the time. But rock & roll has been flamboyant and lavish right from its earliest days and, as for being "in touch," performers never have been; that's merely an illusion. So that criticism doesn't ring true. More likely was the fact that the prog bands—with their superchops, odd time signatures, and long, complex instrumental arrangements—were just seen as being elitist and snobby. But this is a misconception: they really were inventing a new art form and simply wanted to make the best, and most original, music they could. Surely that's the primary objective of any musician?

So, even if progressive rock is not your bag, keep an open mind and you'll find something that will inspire you. One thing's for sure: by studying the riffs and fills in this section, you'll be taking your chops, rhythmic awareness, and musical knowledge to a whole new level.

RIFF NO. 1:

MOODY BLUES STYLE

The Moody Blues' distinctive sound was characterized by their use of the Mellotron (an early tape-loop-based synthesizer), drummer Graeme Edge's poetic interludes, abstract lyrics, and fusions with classical music. In 1967, the Moody Blues released their pivotal album, *Days of Future Passed*, which firmly established them as true "progressive" pioneers and simultaneously heralded the arrival of the progressive rock concept album. In many ways guitarist Justin Hayward provided a foil for the band's more "spaced out" musical extravagances. His melodic playing was never overindulgent and illustrated his strong R&B influences. This example, as well as being harmonically concise, is also fun to play, with its swift position changes making full use of the fretboard.

Justin Hayward performing in 1981.

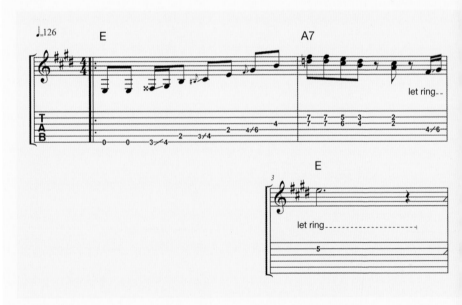

RIFF REGISTER

Technique: Alternate eighth note picking. The double-stop thirds can also be played using hybrid picking.

EDCAG position: Shapes 2 and 3 of the E major scale; double stops from A Mixolydian played along the third and fourth strings.

Harmonic content: When playing over the E chord, the notes used are from E major. For the A7 chord, the A Mixolydian mode is used.

Guitar settings: Middle pickup setting (bridge and neck pickups together).

Amp settings: Select overdrive channel, setting preamp level high.

Effects: None.

WATCH OUT FOR

SHIFTING SMOOTHLY BETWEEN THE NUMEROUS POSITION SHIFTS WITHOUT LOSING THE GROOVE.

A7

RIFF NO. 2:
PINK FLOYD STYLE

Very few progressive rock bands managed to survive the late 1970s. Punk rock made the extravagances of the progressive bands seem unfashionable and uncool against the backdrop of high unemployment and austerity in the UK. Pink Floyd not only survived this period, but went from strength to strength with the release of *The Wall* (1979), which even outsold their earlier masterpiece, *The Dark Side of the Moon* (1973). Guitarist David Gilmour was a master of taste and tone, his bluesy phrasing and licks providing the perfect contrast to Dave Mason's synthesized soundscapes. This example illustrates his minimalist approach: a haunting intro riff built from nothing more than an arpeggiated minor chord.

Pink Floyd in the 1970s.

WATCH OUT FOR
INADVERTENTLY DAMPING THE RINGING OPEN STRINGS BY TOUCHING THEM WITH YOUR FRETTING FINGERS.

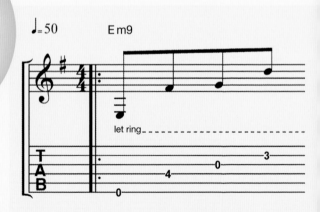

RIFF REGISTER

Technique: Arpeggiated chord played with alternate eighth note picking.

EDCAG position: Em9 chord fretted in shape 2, but adding open strings from shape 1 of Em.

Harmonic content: Tonic minor ninth chord. By placing the ninth (F#) in the same octave as the minor third (G), the chord becomes simultaneously dissonant and consonant.

Guitar settings: Position 4 pickup setting on a Fender Stratocaster.

Amp settings: Select overdrive channel and set preamp level to four o'clock.

Effects: Phaser pedal.

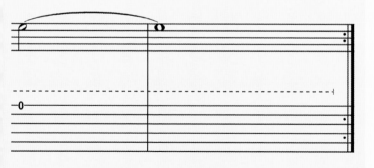

RIFF NO. 3:
YES STYLE

Like Pink Floyd, Yes weathered the late 1970s, but only just; it took a radical change of direction (and band members) in the 1980s to secure their future. Back in the day, nobody had a more complete progressive product than Yes. With surreal album covers courtesy of artist Roger Dean, theatrical stage shows, and numerous concept albums, they were the kings of progressive. The ultimate Yes concept album, *Tales from Topographic Oceans* (1973), was a double album containing just four tracks. Not only was it badly received by critics, but it also led to keyboard whizz Rick Wakeman's departure from the band. However, despite their excesses, Yes have produced some fantastic music: The Yes Album (1971), *Fragile* (1971), and *Close to the Edge* (1972) are rock masterpieces.

Yes performing onstage in 1977.

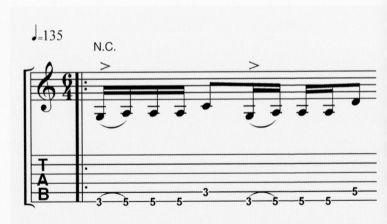

RIFF REGISTER

Technique: Alternate sixteenth note picking, with hammer-ons and quick position shifts.

EDCAG position: Shapes 5 and 1 of the A minor blues scale.

Harmonic content: No chordal accompaniment; rhythmic riff created from tonic blues scale only.

Guitar settings: Bridge pickup with volume and tone up full.

Amp settings: Select overdrive channel, set preamp level to seven o'clock.

Effects: None.

WATCH OUT FOR
GETTING YOUR HEAD AROUND THE 6/4 TIME, WHICH SHOULD BE FELT AS TWO GROUPS OF THREE EIGHTH NOTES AND THREE QUARTER NOTES.

RIFF NO. 4:
GENESIS STYLE

Long before they achieved worldwide pop superstar status, Genesis were a highly respected progressive band on the cutting edge of the trend. Like many progressive guitarists, Genesis' Steve Hackett was as proficient on acoustic guitar as he was on the electric. He frequently recorded with a nylon-string guitar to infuse classical textures into the band's heavily synthesized sound. This example is typical of his approach with Genesis: a short, fingerstyle, pseudo-classical intro that could also function as an interlude section. Don't forget to check the conventional notation if you're mainly reading the TAB—this will tell you which notes should be played with the thumb (stems down) and which with fingers (stems up).

GENESIS

SELLING ENGLAND BY THE POUND

Genesis' *Selling England by the Pound* (1973).

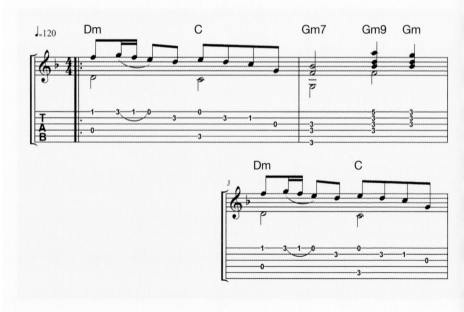

PROGRESSIVE ROCK INTRO RIFFS

RIFF REGISTER

Technique: Conventional fingerpicking technique using the thumb *(p)*, first *(i)*, and second *(m)* fingers of the picking hand.

EDCAG position: Basic open chord shapes in first position.

Harmonic content: Chord sequence diatonic to the D Aeolian (natural minor) scale.

Guitar settings: Acoustic guitar.

Amp settings: N/A.

Effects: N/A.

WATCH OUT FOR

ALWAYS KEEPING A FINGER FREE FOR THE NEXT BASS NOTE. PLAY THE D ON BEAT 2 OF THE FIRST BAR WITH YOUR FOURTH FINGER; THIS LEAVES YOUR THIRD FINGER FREE FOR THE FOLLOWING C BASS NOTE.

Gm   Am7   B♭6   C

RIFF NO. 1:

KING CRIMSON STYLE

Progressive rock guru Robert Fripp launched the first
incarnation of King Crimson in 1969, with the release
of the groundbreaking, platinum-and-gold-selling
In the Court of the Crimson King. Fripp's guitar style
was devoid of blues influences, and this was not only
evident in his playing but also in the band's sound as
a whole. Crimson created a completely new sound that
seemed to come out of nowhere fully formed. Like the
Moody Blues, Crimson used the Mellotron keyboard
to create lush, symphonic sounds. In this example,
jazz and classical influences have been fused to
create a hypnotic sixteenth note arpeggio pattern,
while samples from an original Mellotron provide
suitable ambience.

King Crimson's *In the Court of the
Crimson King* (1969).

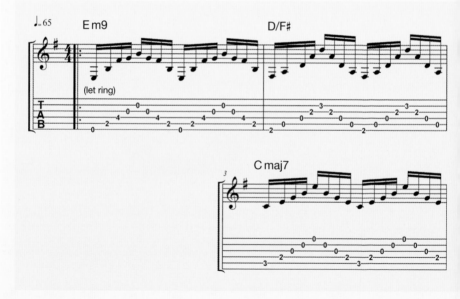

RIFF REGISTER

Technique: Can be played with either alternate sixteenth note picking or economy picking, using the pick to sweep across the strings in one direction.

EDCAG position: Open chord voicings using shape 1 (Em9), shape 4 (D/F#), and shape 3 (Cmaj7 and B7) chords.

Harmonic content: Typical minor chord sequence diatonic to E Aeolian mode, but with the dominant chord (B7) derived from the E harmonic minor scale.

Guitar settings: Neck pickup setting with tone rolled off halfway.

Amp settings: Select clean channel, keeping preamp level low.

Effects: Delay pedal with short to medium repeat; set to low "wet" mix.

WATCH OUT FOR

KEEPING YOUR PICKING EVEN
AND CONSISTENT—FRIPP IS A VERY
PRECISE PLAYER.

B7sus4   B7

RIFF NO. 2:

PINK FLOYD STYLE

This example explores the obligation of every self-respecting progressive band: to play in odd time signatures! This riff is based on a shuffle groove, which adds to the bluesy feel, helping it to sit "in the pocket" so effectively that you barely notice it's in odd time. Generally speaking, most odd time signatures consist of a regular quarter note pulse with time tagged on the end. So, for example, a scary-sounding time signature like 11/8 is nothing more than a bar of 4/4 with three eighth notes added at the end. This example, which is in 7/4, has a heavy drum accent on the seventh beat (with a crash symbol). Therefore, to "feel" the groove correctly, think 6/4 and add an extra quarter note on the end.

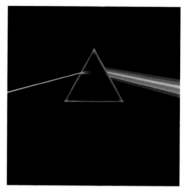

Pink Floyd's *Dark Side of the Moon* (1973).

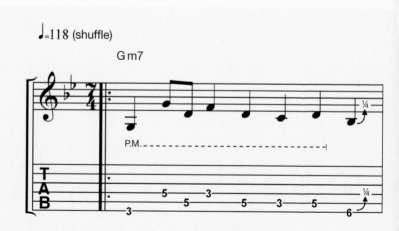

RIFF REGISTER

Technique: Quarter note-based riff played mainly with downpicks.

EDCAG position: Based on shape 1 of the G minor pentatonic scale.

Harmonic content: Minor pentatonic riff highlights all of the important chord tones of the underlying Gm7 harmony.

Guitar settings: Bridge pickup with tone slightly backed off.

Amp settings: Select overdrive channel and set preamp level to five o'clock.

Effects: None.

WATCH OUT FOR

LOSING YOUR PLACE IN THE GROOVE.
THE "EXTRA" NOTE ON THE SEVENTH BEAT IS
ALWAYS ACCENTED BY OMITTING
PALM MUTING.

RIFF NO. 3:

STEVE HILLAGE STYLE

Steve Hillage achieved recognition with psychedelic progressive rock band Gong in the early 1970s. After recording three albums with them, he quit the band in 1975 to pursue a solo career. Hillage combined elements of jazz fusion into his progressive style, adding yet another dimension to the previously classical-influenced genre. This example illustrates this crosspollination of genres with a Mahavishnu-esque style riff. The accents in the notation highlight the start of a repeated four-note pattern that lasts for three beats. Note that it takes three bars to complete its cycle, beginning again on the first beat of the fourth bar if the loop was continued. This technique is known as a polyrhythm—that is, two distinct pulses played simultaneously. The first three bars of the riff are effectively in 3/4, while the drum groove is in 4/4.

Steve Hillage in concert.

RIFF REGISTER

Technique: Alternate eighth note picking accenting the first note of each three-beat grouping.

EDCAG position: Shape 1 of F# Phrygian dominant mode (fifth mode of the harmonic minor scale).

Harmonic content: No chordal accompaniment; polyrhythmic riff created from the dark-sounding Phrygian dominant

mode, with its distinctive minor second interval.

Guitar settings: Bridge pickup with volume and tone up full.

Amp settings: Select overdrive channel, and set preamp level to six o'clock.

Effects: Flange pedal set to medium sweep.

WATCH OUT FOR

FEELING THE ACCENTS OF THE THREE-NOTE GROUPING CONFIDENTLY, SO YOU CAN PLAY IT "IN THE POCKET" WITH FEELING AND GROOVE.

RIFF NO. 4:
JETHRO TULL STYLE

Guitarist Martin Barre joined Jethro Tull in 1968 just before the release of their second album, *Stand Up*. The album was pivotal for the group, establishing what would become their unique style: a fusion of folk, Celtic music, classical music, rock, and blues. However, international superstar status eluded the band until the release of their multi-platinum-selling fourth album, *Aqualung* (1971). This riff showcases the Jethro Tull sound—quintessentially English, with strong folk and medieval music influences clearly audible. The riff involves picking out a melody from the A major chord in the first two bars, and concludes with a descending arpeggiated sequence. A riff like this could be used as a short interlude between vocal refrains, allowing frontman Ian Anderson to double sections of the riff on flute.

Martin Barre performing in the 1970s.

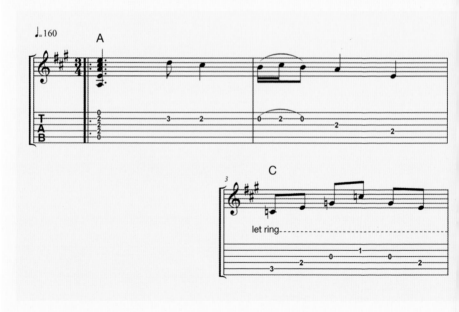

RIFF REGISTER

Technique: Alternate eighth note picking for the melody in the first two bars. Descending arpeggios can also be played with economy picking.

EDCAG position: Single notes based on shape 4 of the A major scale, complemented by shape 3 (C) and shape 5 (G/B) open chords.

Harmonic content: Typically ambiguous folk-flavored chord sequence that shifts from A major to C major/A minor in bar 3.

Guitar settings: Acoustic guitar.

Amp settings: N/A.

Effects: N/A.

WATCH OUT FOR

DAMPING THE NOTES OF THE MELODY WHILE HOLDING DOWN THE A MAJOR CHORD SHAPE. ALWAYS KEEP YOUR FRETTING FINGERS AT A 90-DEGREE ANGLE FROM THE FRETBOARD.

G/B

RIFF NO. 1:

ELP STYLE

Emerson, Lake & Palmer were the world's first progressive rock supergroup. With impeccable progressive credentials, the trio consisted of keyboard virtuoso Keith Emerson, vocalist, bassist, and guitarist Greg Lake, and drummer/percussionist extraordinaire Carl Palmer. The group were unusual for two reasons—first, they were keyboard-led in a guitar-dominated genre; and second, the trio format was rare for progressive bands, testament to Emerson's keyboard prowess that they were able to reproduce their intricate arrangements live. Vocalist and bassist Greg Lake doubled on acoustic and electric guitar in performance and in the studio. This example illustrates his proficient electric guitar skills. Although the riff is played with a wah-wah pedal, it's worth mastering if you don't have one, as the sixteenth note picking is demanding.

Greg Lake performing in 1977.

RIFF REGISTER

Technique: Use the alternate sixteenth note picking as indicated in the TAB, ghosting the unplayed upstrokes to keep the rhythm strong.

EDCAG position: Shape 1/shape 2 E minor pentatonic scale in open position.

Harmonic content: Standard minor pentatonic application over a tonic Em7 chord.

Guitar settings: Bridge pickup with volume rolled off slightly to "clean up" the tone.

Amp settings: Select overdrive channel, keeping preamp level at middle setting.

Effects: Wah-wah pedal.

WATCH OUT FOR

KEEPING THE WAH-WAH PEDAL SWEEPING IN TIME WITH TWO SEPARATE SWEEPS ON THE LOW QUARTER-TONE BENT G NOTES AT THE END OF THE SECOND BAR.

RIFF NO. 2:

MIKE OLDFIELD STYLE

In the early 1970s Richard Branson started his business empire with a small independent record label, Virgin Records, which specialized in signing progressive acts. Mike Oldfield's album *Tubular Bells* (1973) was the label's first release and an immediate smash hit. The multi-platinum-selling debut album established Oldfield as an international megastar. Oldfield played every instrument on the album, a solo progressive rock masterpiece containing just two tracks. This example is typical of his approach—a hypnotic guitar riff that is doubled on bass guitar an octave lower. The riff could be built throughout the song by adding further instrumentation.

Mike Oldfield's *Tubular Bells* (1973).

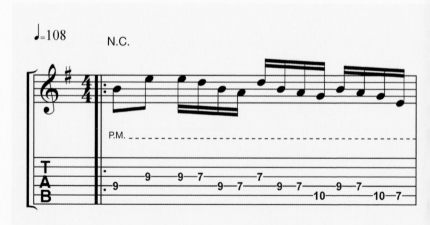

RIFF REGISTER

Technique: Moderately fast alternate sixteenth note picking played across three strings.

EDCAG position: Shape 4 E minor pentatonic.

Harmonic content: Riff constructed entirely from the notes of the minor pentatonic scale.

Guitar settings: Neck pickup with tone rolled off to create a warm, jazzy tone.

Amp settings: Select clean channel, keeping preamp level low and master volume high.

Effects: Flanger pedal.

WATCH OUT FOR
THE TRICKY G MAJOR ARPEGGIO ON THE THIRD BEAT OF THE SECOND BAR. FRET THE LOWEST NOTE (G) WITH YOUR FOURTH FINGER, AS THIS ENSURES YOUR FIRST FINGER REMAINS IN POSITION FOR THE FINAL E NOTE.

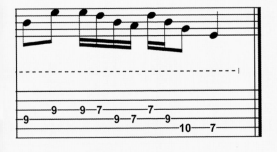

RIFF NO. 3:
FRANK ZAPPA STYLE

The late Frank Zappa was a musical genius—no question. His prolific output of quality music was highly individual, and his acerbic and witty lyrics, orchestral arrangements, and wild guitar solos were an intoxicating mix: you either loved or loathed his music. Zappa's style changed direction many times over the years, but he was always on the cutting edge, an artist truly worthy of the label "progressive." This riff is typical of his mid-1970s period, when he fused rock with just about anything and wasn't afraid to add a few crazy time signatures to boot! Don't forget that odd time signatures usually have a composite note grouping—in this case, 4 + 4 + 4 + 3, as denoted by the sixteenth note beaming. In other words, it's simply a bar of 4/4 with the last sixteenth note omitted.

Frank Zappa in 1971.

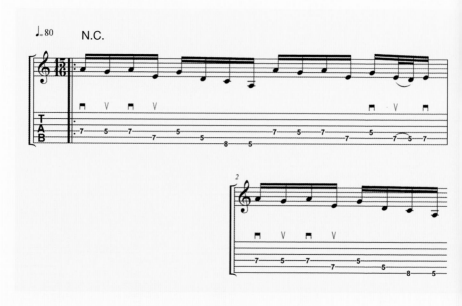

RIFF REGISTER

Technique: Alternate sixteenth note picking but with two "sweeps" required, as indicated in the TAB. This is to ensure that the first note of each bar is always played with a downpick.

EDCAG position: Shape 1 A minor pentatonic scale.

Harmonic content: No chordal accompaniment; unison phrasing.

Guitar settings: Bridge pickup with volume and tone up full.

Amp settings: Select overdrive channel, and set preamp level to five o'clock.

Effects: None.

WATCH OUT FOR

TRYING TO FEEL THE BEAT WITHOUT COUNTING IT, SO YOU CAN RELAX AND GROOVE ON IT!

RIFF NO. 4:
RUSH STYLE

Canadian progressive rockers Rush began their long, illustrious career back in 1974. Early albums betrayed a strong Led Zeppelin influence, but they quickly established their own distinctive sound. With the release of their seventh studio album, *Permanent Waves* (1980), Rush were seeking greater mainstream success and had shortened their songs to make them more "radio-friendly." *Permanent Waves* and the followup, *Moving Pictures* (1981), are widely regarded as their best work, and also represent the peak of the band's commercial success. Guitarist Alex Lifeson's style during this period is encapsulated in this riff, which typifies his inventive and creative approach. By sounding the open first string after each fretted note, a powerful and hypnotic riff is created that is underpinned by the simple descending bass line.

Alex Lifeson performing in 1980.

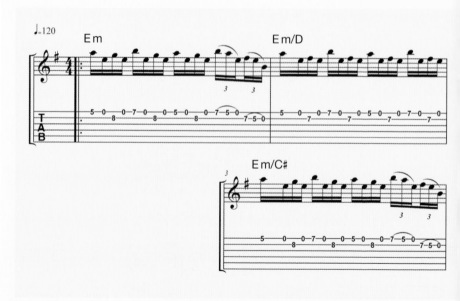

RIFF REGISTER

Technique: Alternate sixteenth note picking with fast sixteenth note triplet pull-offs.

EDCAG position: Based around shape 3 of the E natural minor scale. Can also be viewed as E minor pentatonic with added ninth (F#).

Harmonic content: There are no chords in the accompaniment; the chord symbols simply indicate the implied harmony.

Guitar settings: Bridge pickup with volume backed off slightly.

Amp settings: Select distortion channel, setting preamp levels just above midway.

Effects: Phaser pedal.

WATCH OUT FOR

PLAYING THE SUPER-FAST PULL-OFFS RHYTHMICALLY AND ACCURATELY. FOR BEST RESULTS, RELEASE YOUR FINGERS WITH A SIDEWAYS, FLICKING MOTION.

Em/C   Em/B

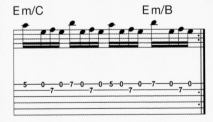

FILL NO. 1:

DAVID GILMOUR STYLE

One of the hallmarks of David Gilmour's playing style is his thick, creamy tone. It's clean but overdriven, overdriven and yet clean; in short, one of the greatest rock guitar tones ever recorded. This elusive tone is very hard to reproduce—proof indeed that it really isn't all about the gear, but about accuracy, touch, sensitivity, use of vibrato, bending in tune, and (most importantly) having musical ideas that are executed with impeccable phrasing. Great players can plug into any old guitar and amp and still sound fantastic. Gilmour's minimalist approach has been reproduced in this fill. It also includes his trademark "double"-bend technique, achieved by bending a note up a tone, releasing it, and then rebending it up a tone and a half. Notice how the fill nestles neatly between two statements of the arpeggiated Em9 chord.

David Gilmour performing in 1977.

WATCH OUT FOR

THE TRICKY DOUBLE BEND IN THE SECOND BAR THAT NEEDS TO HIT THE TARGET NOTES ACCURATELY. LISTEN TO THE CD CAREFULLY, SO YOU CAN HEAR THE PITCHES YOU'RE AIMING FOR.

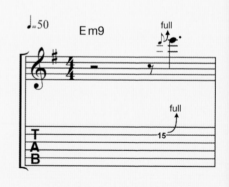

RIFF REGISTER

Technique: Accurate tone and a half bending applied without repicking the note.

EDCAG position: Shape 2 E minor pentatonic scale at the fourteenth fret and an octave lower on the second fret.

Harmonic content: Minor pentatonic lick over Em9 chord. Notice that all of the sustained notes are chord tones (i.e., E, F#, and G).

Guitar settings: Neck pickup with volume and tone on full.

Amp settings: Select overdrive channel, keeping preamp level at around three o'clock.

Effects: None.

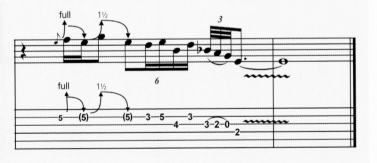

FILL NO. 2:
ROBERT FRIPP STYLE

Robert Fripp's unique and individual playing style bears none
of the trademarks of more conventional rock guitarists. He
purposely avoided rock clichés, choosing instead to draw on
classical and jazz guitarists for his inspiration. In so doing,
he established a distinctive and instantly recognizable style.
It's well worth remembering that it's essential to develop
(and maintain) an eclectic musical taste in order to achieve
individuality. If you want to go one step further and develop
a completely new and original style, then take a leaf out of
Mr. Fripp's book and ignore all the current trends—they are
already established and will soon be out of vogue. It's not
for everybody, and it takes courage and huge amounts of
self-belief, but it's a philosophy that has worked for all of the
great artistic pioneers.

Robert Fripp performing in 1971.

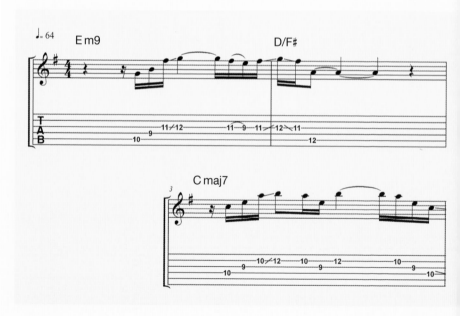

RIFF REGISTER

Technique: Alternate sixteenth note picking played across the strings in arpeggio forms.

EDCAG position: Shape 5 of the tonic E Aeolian (natural minor scale) mode.

Harmonic content: Use of substituted arpeggios to describe extended chord forms (that is, the opening Gmaj7 arpeggio contains all the notes of Em9 bar the root).

Guitar settings: Neck pickup with tone rolled off completely.

Amp settings: Select overdrive channel; set preamp level high.

Effects: None.

WATCH OUT FOR

GIVING IN TO THE TEMPTATION OF USING VIBRATO ON THOSE LONG NOTES! FRIPP PURPOSELY AVOIDED VIBRATO IN ORDER TO SOUND DIFFERENT FROM HIS PEERS.

B7sus4   B7

FILL NO. 3:
STEVE HILLAGE STYLE

When faced with soloing over unusual chords or riffs, most guitar players balk at the thought of wrestling with exotic scales or modes. Often you can get away with simply changing one note of the minor pentatonic, instead—in this instance, the Phrygian dominant mode (mode V of the harmonic minor scale). However, with just one note change the F# minor pentatonic will work just fine. It also means that, with a few tweaks, your favorite pentatonic licks will still work, too! Since there's no second or sixth interval in the minor pentatonic (these are unusually both minor in the Phrygian dominant), the only note that needs to be changed is the minor third. So, raising every A to A# creates a more useable pattern that will get you soloing over this dark and mysterious riff.

Steve Hillage performing with Gong in 2010.

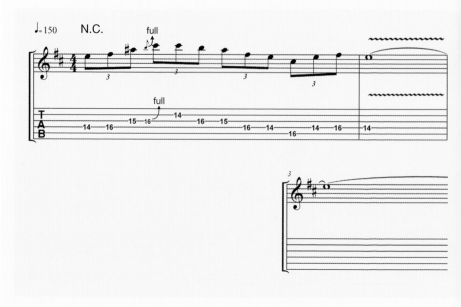

158

RIFF REGISTER

Technique: Alternate eighth note triplet picking with one tone bend in the first bar.

EDCAG position: Shape 1 hybrid F#7 minor/major pentatonic scale.

Harmonic content: Hybrid minor pentatonic creates a useful scale that can be used over any dominant chord.

Guitar settings: Neck pickup with tone backed off a little to "thicken" the sound.

Amp settings: Select overdrive channel, and set preamp level to seven o'clock.

Effects: None.

WATCH OUT FOR

THE QUICK BEND ON THE SECOND BEAT OF THE FIRST BAR—MAKE SURE YOU USE YOUR THIRD FINGER, TO LEAVE YOUR FIRST FINGER IN POSITION FOR THE C# ON THE SECOND STRING.

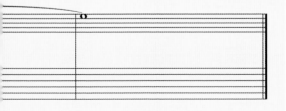

FILL NO. 4:
MIKE OLDFIELD STYLE

Progressive rock musicians were keen to fuse classical concepts with rock music, so many looked to modern classical composers for inspiration. Composers like Stravinsky and Bartók had been using bitonality since the early 20th century, so it also became a popular concept with progressive composers. Bitonality occurs when two different keys are played simultaneously. Mike Oldfield creates his arrangements by multi-tracking different instruments. When he records a lead guitar part, it's likely to be a considered part of the arrangement, just as it is in this example. The underlying riff is based on the notes of the E minor pentatonic scale, so interesting things happen when a fill based on the E major pentatonic scale is overlaid. The whole vibe of the riff lifts and it sounds like a new section.

Mike Oldfield in the studio in 1992.

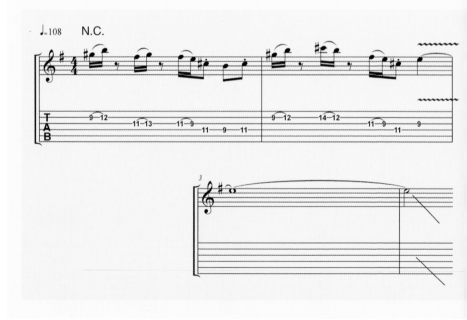

RIFF REGISTER

Technique: Alternate eighth note picking throughout (all of the sixteenth notes are created with hammer-ons and pull-offs).

EDCAG position: Shape 5 of the E major pentatonic scale (the same as shape 1 of C# minor pentatonic).

Harmonic content: Bitonality created by forcing a major pentatonic fill over a minor pentatonic-based riff.

Guitar settings: Bridge pickup with tone backed off slightly.

Amp settings: Select distortion channel, setting preamp levels around six o'clock.

Effects: None.

WATCH OUT FOR

PLAYING THE RESTS—SILENCE IS GOLDEN!
KEEP YOUR HAMMER-ONS AND PULL-OFFS
RHYTHMICALLY ACCURATE.

Matthew Bellamy of Muse performs at the Coachella Music Festival in Indio, California, 2010.

10 KILLER ALTERNATIVE ROCK ALBUMS YOU CAN'T AFFORD TO IGNORE

1 Television • *Marquee Moon* (1977)
2 Talking Heads • *Talking Heads:77* (1977)
3 XTC • *Drums and Wires* (1979)
4 The Smiths • *Hatful of Hollow* (1984)
5 Red Hot Chili Peppers • *Blood Sugar Sex Magik* (1991)
6 R.E.M. • *Automatic for the People* (1992)
7 Radiohead • *Pablo Honey* (1993)
8 Green Day • *Dookie* (1994)
9 Muse • *Absolution* (2003)
10 The Strokes • *Room on Fire* (2003)

ALTERNATIVE ROCK

Alternative rock was a direct descendant of the 1970s punk rock movement. The genre's founders were consequently "left of center" and anti-establishment, shunning the overblown pomposity of "traditional" 1970s rock bands.

Punk rock was not particularly successful from a commercial viewpoint, but it did inspire an entire generation of musicians to get back to the roots of rock & roll. Ever since the 1950s, there had been a relentless pursuit of musical progression in popular music; for many, rock & roll had lost its way back in the 1960s. In the US, the melodically conscious, post-punk, new wave movement included bands such as Talking Heads, Television, and The Cars, whereas in the UK, highly original acts such as XTC, Elvis Costello, and Ian Dury were making new and exciting sounds. New wave was a short-lived genre, however, and by the mid-1980s most of its pioneers had either returned to obscurity or moved with the times and become part of the new "alternative" rock movement.

Born against a backdrop of 1980s synth-pop, and with many of the original new wave musicians on board, alternative rock became one of the few pop-based genres that still championed the electric guitar, and its time came in the early 1990s. Bands such as R.E.M., the Red Hot Chili Peppers, and Green Day—although formed in the previous decade—would now achieve their greatest levels of success.

Whether alternative rock is your thing or not, this inspiring collection of riffs and fills will provide a unique insight into the thinking behind some of rock & roll's most original and interesting musicians.

RIFF NO. 1:
VELVET UNDERGROUND STYLE

Famously bohemian, famously decadent, and famously linked with artist Andy Warhol, the Velvets were the very first alternative rock band, long before the genre even existed. Their hugely influential album *The Velvet Underground & Nico* (1967) is a haunting work. During this period the band featured two guitarists, Lou Reed and Sterling Morrison. This example is a typically atmospheric intro, loosely based on the band's work at this time. A riff such as this would normally be split between the guitarists, one taking the low pedal note, the other playing chords. As you can hear on the track, this also works well when the two independent parts have been arranged for one guitar.

The Velvet Underground (left) with Nico and Andy Warhol in 1965.

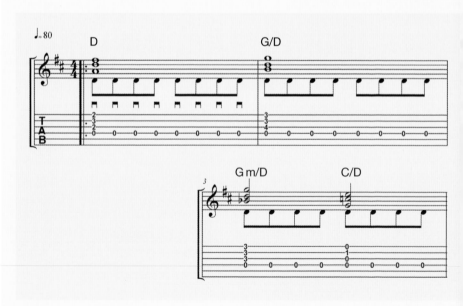

RIFF REGISTER

Technique: Constant downpicks maintaining a steady bass pedal on the fourth string.

EDCAG position: Shape 2 (D), shape 1 (G and Gm), and shape 3 (C) chord.

Harmonic content: Diatonic chords I (D) and IV (G), and non-diatonic chords IVm (Gm) and ♭VII (C), sounded against a constant tonic pedal note.

Guitar settings: Bridge pickup with volume and tone on full.

Amp settings: Select clean channel, keeping preamp level low and output level high.

Effects: None.

WATCH OUT FOR

KEEPING YOUR PICKING CONSTANT AND EVEN. USE DOWNPICKS THROUGHOUT AS INDICATED IN THE TAB.

D

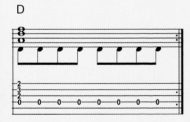

RIFF NO. 2:
THE SMITHS STYLE

Formed in 1982, The Smiths' career spanned just five years. Signed to independent record label Rough Trade, they released a total of four albums, all of which sold in limited quantities outside of the UK. Nonetheless, critics have consistently hailed them as being one of the most important and influential alternative rock bands. Guitarist Johnny Marr's signature sound involved the frequent use of open strings, usually sounded against double stops and chords fretted higher up the neck. Marr also frequently played with a capo; this allowed him to transpose his open string riffs to keys that would suit vocalist Morrissey. The notation for this example effectively ignores the use of the capo, so you can choose whether to play it with or without.

Morrisey and Johnny Marr in 1985.

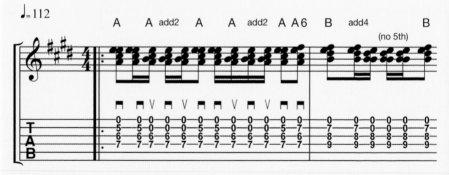

RIFF REGISTER

Technique: Alternate sixteenth note strumming, using ghosted strums to maintain a constant, even rhythm.

EDCAG position: Shape 1 A and B major triads in fifth and seventh positions respectively.

Harmonic content: Droning open strings create complex overtones by sounding the major second (add2) and perfect fourth (add4) against the major third of each triad.

Guitar settings: Neck pickup with volume and tone on full.

Amp settings: Select clean channel, keeping preamp level low and output level high.

Effects: None.

WATCH OUT FOR

INADVERTENTLY DAMPING THE OPEN STRINGS WITH YOUR FIRST OR SECOND FINGERS. KEEP YOUR FINGERS AT 90 DEGREES AGAINST THE FRETBOARD AT ALL TIMES WHEN FRETTING CHORDS.

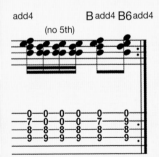

add4 (no 5th)   B add4   B6 add4

RIFF NO. 3:
THE STROKES STYLE

The Strokes' debut album *Is This It* was released in 2001 on a wave of critical acclaim. Interestingly the band are from New York City, USA, but signed to the relaunched UK label Rough Trade, the original mentors of the 1980s alternative and indie scene. The Strokes' lineup features two guitarists, Nick Valensi and Albert Hammond, Jr., on lead and rhythm duties respectively. In this example, a double-stop riff is underpinned by a simple eighth note guitar and bass rhythm in typical Strokes style. The rhythm part has not been notated, but it's very easy to play. You can use either two or three note power chords on the fifth string (play the B5 on the second fret and slide up to the E5 on the seventh fret).

The Strokes' performing in 2006.

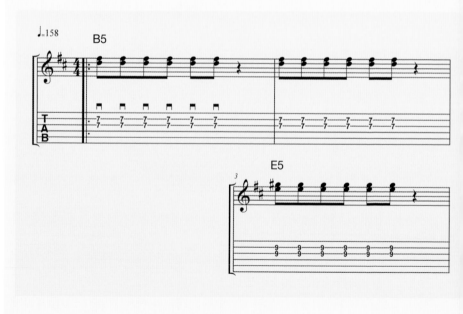

RIFF REGISTER

Technique: Use downpicks throughout to create a strong and consistent delivery.

EDCAG position: Diatonic double stops derived from the B Dorian mode.

Harmonic content: The double-stop riff adds diatonic thirds to the simple power-chord progression, confirming the sequence's minor tonality.

Guitar settings: Bridge pickup with tone backed off a little to tame the treble frequencies.

Amp settings: Select distortion channel, and set preamp level to eight o'clock.

Effects: None.

WATCH OUT FOR

MAKING SURE YOU "PLAY" THE REST ON EVERY FOURTH BEAT. THIS LEAVES SPACE FOR THE SNARE DRUM ON THE BACKBEAT AND SO ENHANCES THE OVERALL GROOVE.

RIFF NO. 4:
R.E.M. STYLE

R.E.M. were the first alternative rock band to achieve global popularity and multi-platinum worldwide sales. While many UK alternative rock bands have struggled to achieve significant sales outside of their home country, R.E.M.'s international success is on a scale that most UK acts could only dream of. Guitarist Peter Buck's unusual style purposely avoided the obvious rock clichés; instead, he drew his influences from folk, 1960s pop music, and punk rock. With an ability to create a riff from little more than a couple of open chords, Buck's unique approach has been captured in this example. Don't be put off by the 6/8 time signature, as this is a common meter for rock ballads and can deliver a wonderfully hypnotic groove.

R.E.M.'s *Automatic for the People* (1992).

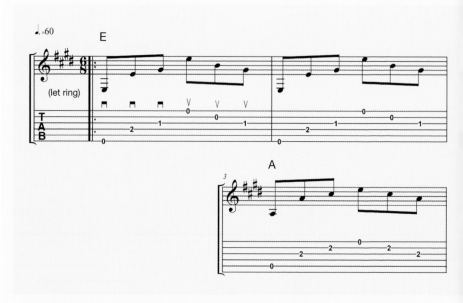

RIFF REGISTER

Technique: Played with the economy picking indicated in the TAB, using consecutive downpicks on descending arpeggios and consecutive up-picks when ascending.

EDCAG position: Shape 1 (E) and shape 4 (A) open position major chords.

Harmonic content: Entirely diatonic to the key of E major. Inclusion of the G note

at the end of the second bar adds sus2 tensions—allow the note to ring into the following bar to resolve.

Guitar settings: Middle pickup setting (neck and bridge pickups).

Amp settings: Select clean channel, keep preamp level low and output level high.

Effects: None.

WATCH OUT FOR

MAINTAINING THAT CONSTANT EIGHTH NOTE PICKING PATTERN. AS ALWAYS, PRACTICING WITH A METRONOME WILL ACHIEVE THE BEST RESULTS.

RIFF NO. 1:

TALKING HEADS STYLE

The post-punk, new wave movement of the late 1970s directly influenced the alternative rock movement of the 1980s. In effect these bands were alternative rock—it's just that the genre hadn't been invented yet! David Byrne's guitar work represented a brave departure from the slick AOR, mainstream guitar styles that dominated the airwaves at the time. The band's raw, seemingly unprocessed sound was unfussy and direct; however, like all successful rock & roll bands, the guitar parts were carefully constructed and often multi-tracked to create exciting grooves, just as in this example. The parts have been panned hard right and left, so to hear either part in detail, simply adjust the balance control of your audio playback device.

David Byrne performing onstage.

RIFF REGISTER

Technique: Alternate picked arpeggios in guitar one; downpicked double stops in guitar two.

EDCAG position: Guitar one is based on simple shape 4, 3, and 5 open chords; guitar two picks out the top notes of a shape 1 major barre.

Harmonic content: By substituting a dominant seventh chord for the tonic major,

the riff achieves an ambiguous, bluesy quality.

Guitar settings: Guitar one, bridge middle pickup (neck and bridge); guitar two, bridge pickup.

Amp settings: Guitar one, clean channel; guitar two, overdrive channel.

Effects: Chorus pedal on guitar one only.

WATCH OUT FOR

USING DOWNPICKS FOR ALL THE QUARTER NOTE CHORDS IN GUITAR TWO. MANY PLAYERS WRONGLY ASSUME THAT CHORDS PLAYED ON THE BACKBEAT SHOULD BE PLAYED WITH AN UP-PICK.

RIFF NO. 2:

XTC STYLE

While Talking Heads spearheaded the new wave movement in the US, XTC were the UK's equivalent pioneers. With a lineup that featured two guitarists—Andy Partridge and Dave Gregory—the band strived to create new and original sounds that shunned the accepted clichés of 1970s rock music. Their most successful album, *English Settlement*, was also arguably the band's best recording. Released in 1982, it also officially established the band as part of the 1980s alternative rock scene. This example focuses on the choppy, vibrant rhythm style of vocalist-songwriter-guitarist Andy Partridge. This simple four-bar example provides the perfect accompaniment for a verse section.

XTC performing onstage in 1980.

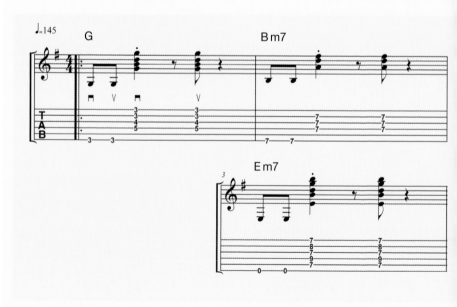

RIFF REGISTER

Technique: Alternate eighth note picking on chords and single notes. Follow the picking indicated in the TAB for best results.

EDCAG position: Shape 1 (G and Bm7) and shape 4 (Em7) barre chords.

Harmonic content: Diatonic I–III–VI progression in the key of G major. Notice the tasty "contrary motion" in the first two bars (i.e., bass rises, while top note falls, in second bar).

Guitar settings: Bridge pickup with volume and tone on full.

Amp settings: Select overdrive channel, setting preamp level at around six o'clock.

Effects: None.

WATCH OUT FOR

FRETTING THE BM7 CHORD CORRECTLY: USE YOUR THIRD FINGER TO FORM A SEMI-BARRE ACROSS THE HIGHER STRINGS WHILE YOUR SECOND FINGER FRETS THE BASS NOTE.

RIFF NO. 3:

RADIOHEAD STYLE

Although the band originally formed in 1985, all of the members were still at school. They remained together right through their school and university years, rehearsing and performing at weekends. It wasn't until the early 1990s—with degrees safely under their belts—that they could concentrate fully on their musical career. By 1992 they had already signed a six-album deal with EMI Records and the following year released their debut album, *Pablo Honey*. The album went platinum in both the UK and US, a considerable achievement for a debut release. All of their albums have also achieved platinum status, confirming the band as one of the biggest alternative rock acts in the world, second only to R.E.M. This simple, yet effective, acoustic riff is typical of the band's early 1990s work.

Jonny Greenwood performing in 2008.

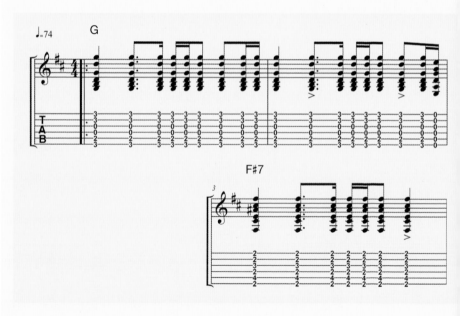

RIFF REGISTER

Technique: Use alternate sixteenth note strumming throughout, ghosting the pick above the strings when it's not sounding the strings.

EDCAG position: Open shape 5 (G) and shape 4 (A6) chords mixed with shape 1 (F#7) and shape 4 (Bm) barre chords.

Harmonic content: By starting the riff on the VI chord (G in the key of Bm), the tonality effectively remains ambiguous throughout.

Guitar settings: N/A.

Amp settings: N/A.

Effects: None.

WATCH OUT FOR

KEEPING YOUR STRUMMING LIGHT AND CONSISTENT, ADDING SLIGHT BACKBEAT ACCENTS AS INDICATED IN THE SECOND BAR.

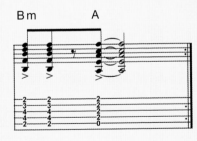

RIFF NO. 4:
THE CURE STYLE

Long-running alternative rock band The Cure have survived not only changing fashions but also frequent lineup changes. So many personnel have come and gone, in fact, that vocalist-guitarist-songwriter Robert Smith remains the only founder member. Their debut album, *Imaginary Boys* (1979), placed them firmly in the post-punk, new wave movement on its release. But, like XTC, as the genre waned in the 1980s, the band moved with the times and today are widely regarded as true alternative rock pioneers. Smith's guitar style is concise and effective, its primary purpose to accompany and support rather than to display technical prowess. In this example, in typically Smith-esque style, a simple, yet melodic, arpeggiated picking pattern creates a weaving melody line in the verse section.

Robert Smith performing in 1987.

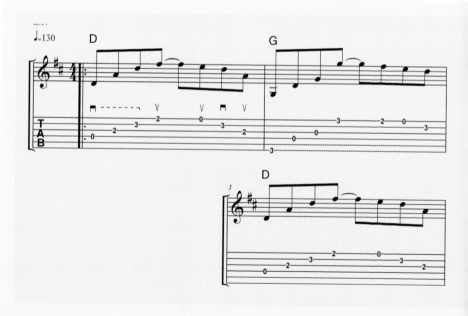

ALTERNATIVE ROCK VERSE RIFFS

RIFF REGISTER

Technique: Can be played with alternate eighth note picking or with the semi-economy downpicking as indicated in the TAB.

EDCAG position: Shape 2 (D), shape 5 (G), and shape 4 (A7) open position major chords.

Harmonic content: Entirely diatonic to the key of D major. However, inclusion of non-chord notes creates temporary dissonance in the moving melodic lines.

Guitar settings: Bridge pickup setting with tone backed off slightly.

Amp settings: Select clean channel, keeping preamp level low and output level high.

Effects: Chorus pedal.

WATCH OUT FOR

ALLOWING ALL THE NOTES TO RING FOR THEIR FULL VALUE—KEEP NOTES FRETTED FOR THEIR FULL VALUE AND WHEREVER POSSIBLE ALLOW OPEN STRINGS TO RING ON.

A 7

RIFF NO. 1:

GREEN DAY STYLE

Green Day took the simplistic style of punk rock, added vocal hooks with pop sensibility, then dialed in a carefully produced, fat guitar sound. It was a winning formula that made them one of the most popular alternative rock bands of the 1990s. Ever since the release of their third album, *Dookie* (1994), which achieved diamond status in the USA, all of their albums have achieved multi-platinum sales. Guitarist-vocalist-songwriter Billie Joe Armstrong is famous for his huge guitar sound, achieved by playing his famous Gibson Les Paul Junior through that most ubiquitous of rock amps, the Marshall stack. Taking a leaf out of the books of classic rock and heavy metal guitarists, Billie double tracks his rhythm parts. These are panned hard right and left to create that trademark "monster" rhythm sound.

Billie Joe Armstrong performing in 2009.

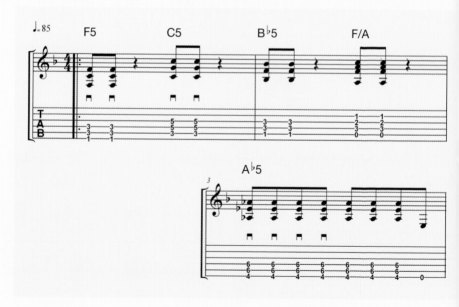

RIFF REGISTER

Technique: Constant downpicks throughout create a fat, authoritative rhythm sound.

EDCAG position: Shape 1 and shape 4 power chords (F5, C5, and B♭5) mixed with shape 1 full major chords (F/A and G).

Harmonic content: The first inversion F chord (F/A) facilitates a smooth movement to the non-diatonic A♭. While the root note falls chromatically, the top note of both chords (C) remains constant.

Guitar settings: Bridge pickup with volume and tone up full.

Amp settings: Select overdrive channel, setting preamp level around eight o'clock.

Effects: None.

WATCH OUT FOR

KEEPING STRING NOISE TO A MINIMUM DURING THE RESTS; ACHIEVE IT BY DAMPING THE STRINGS BETWEEN CHORD HITS WITH YOUR PICKING HAND.

G5   C5

RIFF NO. 2:
MUSE STYLE

English alternative rockers Muse have been described
as new progressive, space rock, symphonic rock, and
progressive metal! This wide range of associated styles
illustrates how original and eclectic their output has been
since the release of their debut album, *Showbiz*, in 1999.
This riff is based entirely on two note power chords. Many
guitar players have a "favorite" power-chord shape and
usually stick to it. However, because this riff is played
at a much brighter tempo with a constant eighth note
rhythm, the two note variant is easier to move around the
neck quickly. It also produces a tighter sound. So don't
just let your fingers decide: next time you're playing
power chords, consider which shape will be best fit for
your purpose!

Matthew Bellamy performing in 2011.

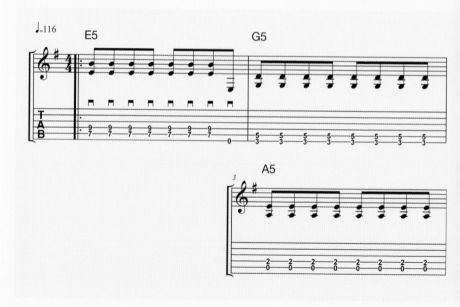

RIFF REGISTER

Technique: Constant downpicks are used throughout to create a consistent delivery.

EDCAG position: Shape 4 (E5) and shape 1 (G5, A5, C5, and B5) power chords.

Harmonic content: A chord progression diatonic to the E Aeolian mode. Although there are no thirds in the chords, the root movement of the sequence effectively establishes the minor key.

Guitar settings: Bridge pickup with volume and tone on full.

Amp settings: Select overdrive channel, and set preamp level at around nine o'clock.

Effects: None.

WATCH OUT FOR

MOVING QUICKLY AND SMOOTHLY BETWEEN CHORDS. NOTICE HOW THE OPEN SIXTH STRING FACILITATES THE QUICK CHANGE TO THE G5 IN THE SECOND BAR.

C5   B5

RIFF NO. 3:
RED HOT CHILI PEPPERS STYLE

The long and checkered career of the Red Hot Chili Peppers began in California in 1983. The band's lineup has featured several guitar players (including original member, Hillel Slovak, who died of a heroin overdose), but the longest-serving player, and the one most associated with the classic Chili's lineup, is John Frusciante. Frusciante played on the group's most critically acclaimed albums, *Blood Sugar Sex Magik* (1991) and *Californication* (1999). His style—a blend of classic rock, funk, and punk—ranges from aggressive and hard-edged to subtle and sensitive. This example is based on Frusciante's approach in the early 1990s, during the band's funkiest period. It's a heavily syncopated riff and quite demanding, so start slowly and build up speed gradually to ensure rhythmic accuracy is always maintained.

The Red Hot Chili Peppers in 1989.

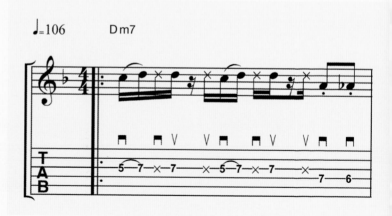

RIFF REGISTER

Technique: Use alternate sixteenth note strumming throughout, using your fretting hand to create the percussive notes (touching the string with your finger but without pressing it onto the fingerboard).

EDCAG position: Shape 4 D minor blues scale riff that incorporates a shape 2 G7 voicing.

Harmonic content: Essentially a II–V (Dm7–G7) vamp, with the guitar harmonizing

the climbing bass notes in thirds at the end of the second bar.

Guitar settings: Position 4 (neck and middle pickups) selector setting on a Fender Strat.

Amp settings: Select overdrive channel but keep preamp level low, at around 3 o'clock.

WATCH OUT FOR

PICKING THE NOTES FIRMLY BUT ACCURATELY WHILE AVOIDING SOUNDING ANY ADJACENT STRINGS.

G7sus4   G7

RIFF NO. 4:

JANE'S ADDICTION STYLE

Jane's Addiction formed in 1985 and released just two albums, *Nothing's Shocking* (1988) and *Ritual de lo Habitual* (1990), before disbanding in 1991. They later reformed (although not as the original lineup) in 1997 and to date have released a further two albums. Their original debut album was a big influence on the (then) still new alternative rock scene. Dave Navarro's fiery, metal-flavored riffs brought a harder and much rockier sound to a previously jangly, pop-influenced genre. This riff is in keeping with Navarro's style during the late 1980s. Using two note power chords high up the neck makes sliding between chords much easier, and this is used to good effect in the riff. By incorporating the low, palm-muted, open E, the riff is given extra weight and authority.

Dave Navarro performing in 1997.

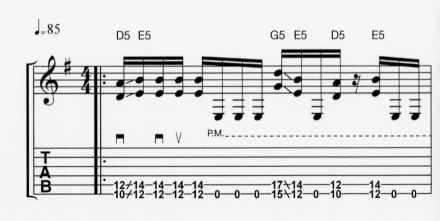

RIFF REGISTER

Technique: Alternate sixteenth note strumming throughout. As only the fifth and sixth strings are sounded, keep strum sweep narrow—this allows for greater accuracy and consistency.

EDCAG position: Shape 1, two note and three note power chords played based around the E5 on the 12th fret.

Harmonic content: Entirely diatonic to the key of E minor, with chords derived form the E Aeolian mode.

Guitar settings: Bridge pickup setting with volume and tone on full.

Amp settings: Select distortion channel and set preamp level around eight o'clock.

WATCH OUT FOR

USING CONTROLLED PALM MUTING; ONLY THE OPEN SIXTH STRING MUST BE MUTED. RELEASE YOUR PALM QUICKLY TO AVOID CHOKING THE CHORDS.

FILL NO. 1:
ADDING OUTRO FILLS

Alternative rock arose from the ashes of the punk rock
movement, and therefore retained its anti-guitar solo
ethic—for this reason, most alternative rock bands don't
feature guitar solos. When solos do appear, they are less
likely to be improvised and more likely to be carefully
constructed, to enhance the song. In many ways this makes
the proposition of adding fills more challenging: they must
always serve the song and can never sound flashy. In this
example, we've taken alternative rock Intro riff no. 4 from
the start of the chapter and placed it in an outro setting. In
this situation, the fill's purpose is to add weight and depth,
pushing the song to its natural conclusion. Notice how the
long, sustained root notes effectively bolster the sequence
but still leave plenty of space for the vocals.

Peter Buck of R.E.M. in 1995.

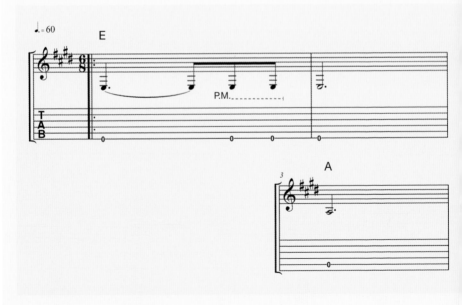

ALTERNATIVE ROCK FILLS

RIFF REGISTER

Technique: Alternate eighth note picking incorporating a single pull-off and slide in the fourth bar.

EDCAG position: Shape 2 E Mixolydian mode-based riff.

Harmonic content: By using the Mixolydian mode, suspended fourth tensions (D to C#) can effectively be added in the final bar over the A chord.

Guitar settings: Bridge pickup with volume and tone up full.

Amp settings: Select overdrive channel, setting preamp level around six o'clock.

Effects: None.

WATCH OUT FOR

PREVENTING THE LOW OPEN STRINGS FROM RINGING INTO EACH OTHER. ALSO BE CAREFUL TO MUTE THE OPEN A BEFORE PLAYING THE DESCENDING LINE IN THE FOURTH BAR.

FILL NO. 2:
ADDING VERSE FILLS

Adding fills while observing the alternate rock ethic of "no guitar solos" is not easy. However, as we've already established in other genres, the sole purpose of a fill is to provide additional interest, but it must always be subservient to the vocal melody. In this example, a simple double-stop idea is repeated against the G and Bm7 chords. Short ideas like this always work really well when they are repeated, unchanged, against the next chord in the sequence. Often the best way to come up with simple riffs like this is to base your ideas around the tonic scale and ignore the chord changes. Chances are, if your idea works well against the tonic chord, it should also work over any other diatonic chords in the sequence.

XTC's *Drums and Wires* (1979).

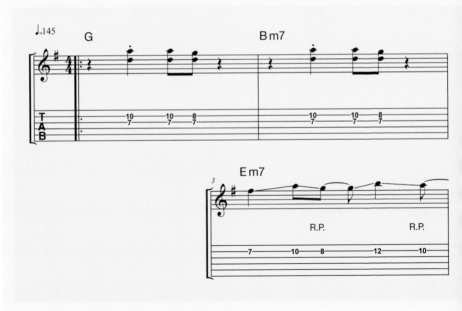

RIFF REGISTER

Technique: Use downpicks for an aggressive double-stop riff and strong pitches when sliding single notes along the second string.

EDCAG position: Shape 3 (G major scale) double-stop riff. Sliding line shifts along the second string through shapes 3, 4, and 5 of the tonic scale.

Harmonic content: The G still works against the Bm7 in the second bar (even though it potentially clashes with the F# in the chord) because the tonic key (G major) has already been established.

Guitar settings: Neck pickup with tone rolled off to create a fat, "bell-like" tone.

Amp settings: Select distortion channel, and set preamp level at around seven o'clock.

R.P.

WATCH OUT FOR

BEING TEMPTED TO ADD VIBRATO TO THAT FINAL, LONG B NOTE. REMEMBER: YOU SHOULD ALWAYS BE TRYING TO AVOID OBVIOUS CLICHÉD APPROACHES!

FILL NO. 3:

BILLIE JOE ARMSTRONG STYLE

Soloing in a power trio setting, just like Green Day's vocalist-guitarist Billie Joe Armstrong, presents its own set of challenges. Fills can easily be overdubbed in the studio along with other multi-tracked parts, but in a live situation it's essential to fill out the sound, as there will be no rhythm part to support you. Jimi Hendrix faced the same problem, as did Eric Clapton in Cream: Jimi added double stops and triads to his solos to fill out the sound, while Eric relied on sheer volume and raw blues power. Billie Joe took a different route, by pioneering the use of octaves, played along the strings. It's an approach that effectively creates a full, fat sound (especially when the octaves are strummed, as in this example) that is ideal for creating dense, dramatic fills and licks.

Billie Joe Armstrong performing in 2010.

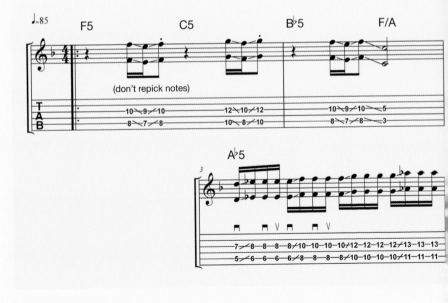

RIFF REGISTER

Technique: Pick only the first note of each slide in the first two bars, but use alternate sixteenth note strumming in bars 3 and 4.

EDCAG position: Linear fill that descends through shapes 4 and 2 of the F major scale, then ascends through shapes 5, 1, 2, and 3 of the C harmonic minor scale in bars 3 and 4.

Harmonic content: The first two bars are rooted in F major territory. In bars 3 and 4, the A♭ and implied G major chord suggest a modulation to C minor—hence the use of the C harmonic minor scale.

Guitar settings: Bridge pickup with volume and tone on full.

Amp settings: Select overdrive channel, setting preamp level high at around eight o'clock.

WATCH OUT FOR

DAMPING ALL OF THE STRINGS THAT YOU'RE NOT FRETTING. ANGLE YOUR FIRST FINGER SO THAT THE TIP DAMPS THE SIXTH STRING AND THE FIRST JOINT RESTS ACROSS THE REMAINING STRINGS (WITHOUT FRETTING).

G5   C5

```
-13⁓16—16—16—16—16⁓17----------------
-11⁓14—14—14—14—14⁓15----------------
```

FILL NO. 4:
JOHN FRUSCIANTE STYLE

John Frusciante's style, like that of many players, is firmly rooted in an obsession with all things analog and old school. He famously plays a vintage Fender Stratocaster and regularly uses a wide range of original 1970s effects, including chorus, distortion, wah-wah, delay, flanger, and octave pedals. He's a firm believer in emotive guitar playing and is well known for his dislike of fast, technical players and shredding. In this example, one-bar fills are added in the second bar of each two-bar funk riff. The combination of a wah-wah pedal (sweeping in time with the quarter note pulse) and percussive, muted notes creates effective and very funky phrases that "sit in the pocket" perfectly. If you don't have a wah-wah pedal, it's still worth checking out this fill, as it contains strong sixteenth note phrasing ideas.

John Frusciante performing in the 1990s.

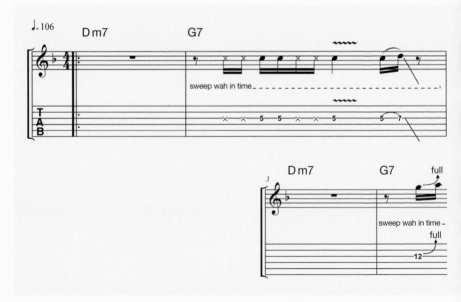

RIFF REGISTER

Technique: Alternate sixteenth picking combined with picking-hand muting, achieved by releasing the pressure of your finger without releasing from the string.

EDCAG position: Shape 4 and shape 1 D minor blues scale.

Harmonic content: The chord sequence is a II–V vamp (Dm7–G7). This sequence can always be negotiated with the minor

blues (or minor pentatonic) scale, starting on the II chord's root note, as in this example.

Guitar settings: Bridge pickup setting with volume and tone on full.

Amp settings: Select distortion channel and set preamp level at around six o'clock.

Effects: Wah-wah pedal.

WATCH OUT FOR

KEEPING THE WAH-WAH PEDAL SWEEPING IN TIME WHILE YOU PLAY THE LICK—THIS MAY TAKE A LITTLE PRACTICE, BUT IT'S A COOL TECHNIQUE THAT'S WELL WORTH THE EFFORT.

John McLaughlin
performing in Boston,
Massachusetts, in 1973.

10 KILLER FUSION ALBUMS
YOU CAN'T AFFORD TO IGNORE

1 Miles Davis • *Bitches Brew* (1970)
2 Mahavishnu Orchestra • *The Inner Mounting Flame* (1971)
3 Billy Cobham • *Spectrum* (1973)
4 Soft Machine • *Bundles* (1975)
5 Jeff Beck • *Wired* (1976)
6 Bruford • *Feels Good to Me* (1978)
7 Mike Stern • *Upside Downside* (1986)
8 Chick Corea • *The Chick Corea Elektric Band* (1986)
9 Pat Metheny Group • *Still Life (Talking)* (1987)
10 Morrissey–Mullen • *Happy Hour* (1988)

FUSION

The origins of fusion can be traced back to the late 1960s and the pioneering work of jazz genius Miles Davis. It was his "all electric" jazz albums *In a Silent Way* (1969) and *Bitches Brew* (1970) that are widely considered to be the most influential and earliest fusion recordings.

By the early 1970s, jazz rock was fully established and enjoyed considerable popularity until jazz funk's rise to prominence in the late 1970s. The roots of jazz funk can be traced back to the work of James Brown, guitarist Grant Green, and keyboardist Herbie Hancock. It was a mellower sound, with a strong backbeat, and enjoyed considerable commercial success during the 1980s, with mainstream acts such as Sade, Level 42, and Shakatak even enjoying a high level of singles chart success. The 1980s jazz rock fusion label was shortened to "fusion" in the interests of brevity, so it is this period that is most widely associated with the genre. Prominent pioneers of 1980s fusion included Miles Davis, Tribal Tech, Chick Corea's Elektric Band, John Scofield, and Mike Stern.

Fusion remains alive and well to this day and many important fusion musicians like Mike Stern, Allan Holdsworth, and John Scofield have remained loyal to the genre that launched their careers. Fusion is not an obvious music—it was never intended to be—and so many listeners are put off by its seemingly ostentatious and elitist stance. However, dig a little deeper and you'll be rewarded with some of the finest music that has ever been recorded. Regardless of your musical preferences, prepare to have your sense of harmony and time stretched to the max with this eclectic collection of challenging fusion riffs and fills.

RIFF NO. 1:
JOHN MCLAUGHLIN STYLE

John McLaughlin is considered by many to be the king of fusion guitar. He rose to prominence after joining the Miles Davis Group in 1969, but is most widely associated with 1970s fusion outfit Mahavishnu Orchestra, led by McLaughlin and featuring keyboard wizard Jan Hammer and virtuoso drummer Billy Cobham. The group was a huge influence on the popular 1970s jazz rock movement. Famed for his incredibly fast single-note lines, McLaughlin is also a gifted composer. This example illustrates his use of polyrhythms (where two non-related rhythms are played simultaneously): by using groupings of three eighth notes, the riff appears to float across the underlying 4/4 pulse, finally slotting back into the groove in the third bar.

John McLaughlin performing in 1988.

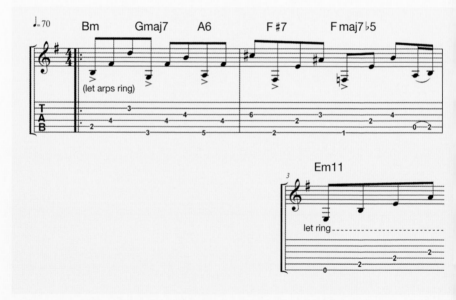

FUSION MEGA RIFFS

RIFF REGISTER

Technique: Alternate eighth note picking with strong, confident, offbeat accents.

EDCAG position: Shape 4 (Bm) and shape 1 three note chord voicings.

Harmonic content: The non-diatonic F#7 and Fmaj7♭5 chords in the second bar add harmonic interest, and the chromatic root movement also pulls the sequence home to the tonic chord.

Guitar settings: Neck pickup with volume and tone up full.

Amp settings: Select overdrive channel, and set preamp level around five o'clock.

Effects: Envelope filter (auto wah-wah).

WATCH OUT FOR

PLAYING THIS CONFIDENTLY (AND IN TIME) OVER A 4/4 PULSE. YOU CAN ONLY DO THIS IF YOU PRACTICE WITH A 4/4 GROOVE (USE A DRUM MACHINE OR A LOOP IN YOUR SEQUENCING SOFTWARE).

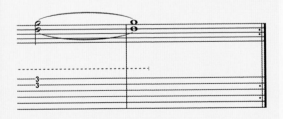

RIFF NO. 2:
JEFF BECK STYLE

Considered by many to be the ultimate guitarists' guitarist, Beck has inspired and amazed an army of loyal followers since his early days with the Yardbirds in the 1960s. In the 1970s, he recorded two highly influential and critically acclaimed fusion albums with ex-Beatles producer George Martin—*Blow by Blow* (1975) and *Wired* (1976). This riff is loosely based on Beck's work during this period and highlights his tight, controlled, but extremely funky style. Beck famously doesn't use a pick when he plays, preferring to use his thumb and fingers instead. Although this riff can be played with a pick, a more relaxed and musical performance can be achieved with hybrid picking.

Jeff Beck performing on TV in 1975.

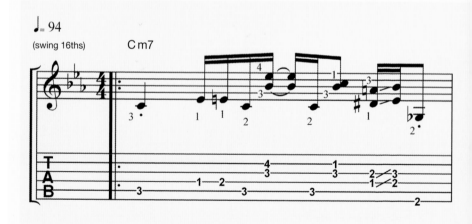

FUSION MEGA RIFFS

RIFF REGISTER

Technique: Can be played fingerstyle or using hybrid picking—picking the notes on the second string with your third finger (a) and the notes on the third string with your second finger (m).

EDCAG position: Shape 3 C Dorian/C Mixolydian-based riff.

Harmonic content: Cm7-based riff

includes the major third to heighten the movement to the following F7 chord.

Guitar settings: Bridge pickup with volume rolled off slightly.

Amp settings: Select distortion channel, setting preamp level at around six o'clock.

Effects: None.

WATCH OUT FOR

FOR BEST RESULTS, USE THE FINGERING INDICATED IN THE NOTATION. HOWEVER, DON'T BE AFRAID TO EXPERIMENT WITH ALTERNATIVES SUCH AS USING YOUR THUMB FOR THE SIXTH-STRING NOTES.

F7

RIFF NO. 3:

JIM MULLEN STYLE

Jim Mullen is one of the UK's fusion legends. Along with the late saxophonist Dick Morrissey, he formed Morrissey–Mullen in the mid-1970s, a band that influenced the emerging jazz funk scene enormously. They recorded a total of eight albums between 1976 and 1988, after which Mullen departed to pursue a solo career that moved more into "straight ahead" jazz territory. Mullen's soulful, bluesy style is highly individual, due in part to his preference for playing entirely with his thumb. In this example, double stops are used to create an intricate, melodic riff over harmonically unrelated chords. Melody and phrasing are pivotal to his technique—undoubtedly one of the main reasons why he has remained one of the UK's most popular jazz and fusion guitarists.

Jim Mullen performing in 1977.

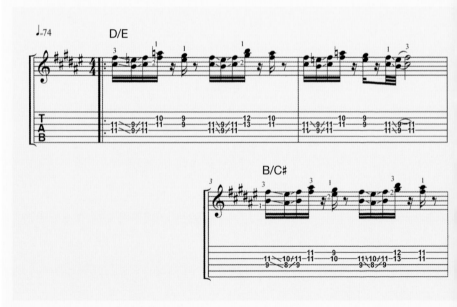

FUSION MEGA RIFFS

RIFF REGISTER

Technique: Can be played "Mullen style" by strumming the double stops with your thumb. You may prefer to use conventional pick technique, which also works perfectly.

EDCAG position: Shape 5 E Mixolydian mode in bars 1 and 2, shape 1 C# Mixolydian mode in bars 3 and 4.

Harmonic content: The relevant Mixolydian mode is applied to each chord,

but in the same neck position. Common tones are created, effectively connecting two unrelated chords.

Guitar settings: Neck pickup with tone backed off to around 75 percent.

Amp settings: Select clean channel, keeping preamp level low and output high.

Effects: None.

WATCH OUT FOR

PLAYING THE DOUBLE-STOP SLIDES CLEANLY AND RHYTHMICALLY. FOR BEST RESULTS, USE THE FINGERING INDICATED.

RIFF NO. 4:
MIKE STERN STYLE

Mike Stern burst onto the jazz fusion scene in the mid-1980s, fresh from touring and recording with the legendary Miles Davis Group. His spacey, chorused sound provided lush clean jazz tones juxtaposed against an out-and-out distorted solo sound. He mixed complex bebop lines with screaming blues licks in the same solo; no fusion guitarist had mixed the two styles so bravely and effectively before Stern. Stern has an incredibly individual style and sound, in part achieved by mixing the sounds he loved from the disparate worlds of jazz and rock. This riff is typical of Stern's style: a bluesy, heavily syncopated riff played in unison with the bass against a driving drum groove.

Mike Stern performing in 2010

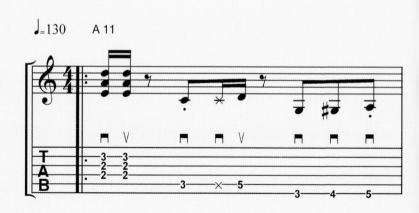

RIFF REGISTER

Technique: Alternate sixteenth picking with muted notes (created by releasing the pressure of your fretting hand).

EDCAG position: Shape 5 and shape 1 A minor blues scale.

Harmonic content: From the opening suspended chord, this riff is designed to sound harmonically ambiguous. However, basing the riff on the blues scale retains a strong sense of tonality.

Guitar settings: Neck pickup setting with tone backed off slightly.

Amp settings: Select clean channel, keeping preamp level low and output high.

Effects: Chorus pedal.

WATCH OUT FOR

PLAYING THE RIFF WITH RHYTHMIC ACCURACY. USE ALTERNATE SIXTEENTH NOTE PICKING, GHOSTING THE PICK ABOVE THE STRINGS DURING RESTS AND LONGER NOTES.

N.C.

RIFF NO. 1:
SOFT MACHINE STYLE

Soft Machine's second album, *Volume Two* (1969), was a pioneering and influential jazz fusion release. In 1975 they released another pivotal recording, *Bundles*, their seventh album. This was their first release featuring an electric guitarist in the lineup, changing the band's sound, giving them a harder, rockier edge. The guitarist was the then unknown Allan Holdsworth, who dominated the recording with his dazzling flurries of fast legato single lines. To this day he remains one of the genre's most important and influential players. This example is representative of the Soft Machine sound during the "Holdsworth" period, a rock-influenced, blues-flavored fusion riff in 6/8 time.

Soft Machine's *Bundles* (1975).

WATCH OUT FOR

PLAYING THIS CONFIDENTLY (AND IN TIME) OVER THE UNUSUAL 6/8 PULSE. THE RIFF HAS A FULL "SIX-TIME" FEEL—THERE'S NO UNDERLYING TWO PULSE AS THERE WOULD BE IN A 6/8 BLUES OR A ROCK BALLAD.

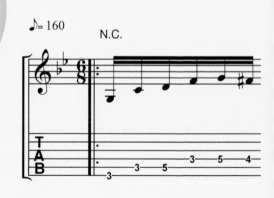

FUSION ODD TIME RIFFS

RIFF REGISTER

Technique: Alternate sixteenth note picking. Because the riff is played in 6/8 time, remember that the main pulse is an eighth note, so sixteenth notes will effectively feel like eighths.

EDCAG position: Shape 1 G minor blues scale.

Harmonic content: Since there are no accompanying chords, this riff has an

ambiguous bluesy flavor. It could be harmonized by either dominant seventh or minor seventh chords.

Guitar settings: Bridge pickup with volume and tone up full.

Amp settings: Select overdrive channel, and set preamp level around eight o'clock.

Effects: None.

RIFF NO. 2:

BILLY COBHAM STYLE

Billy Cobham has been described as "fusion's greatest drummer." He found fame and critical recognition recording and touring with Miles Davis in the early 1970s, and in 1971 co-founded the Mahavishnu Orchestra with John McLaughlin. He released his first solo recording in 1973, the hugely influential album *Spectrum*. This was full of Cobham's heavyweight compositions, including the famous "Stratus" and "Red Barron." This example is in typical Cobham style, a heavily syncopated riff in 7/8 time. Cobham's take on the 7/8 groove was simply to treat it as a bar of 4/4 with the last eighth note removed. In other words, you still get the backbeat snare, but the first beat feels like a pushed offbeat.

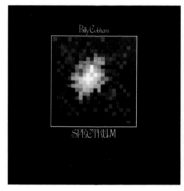

Billy Cobham's *Spectrum* (1973).

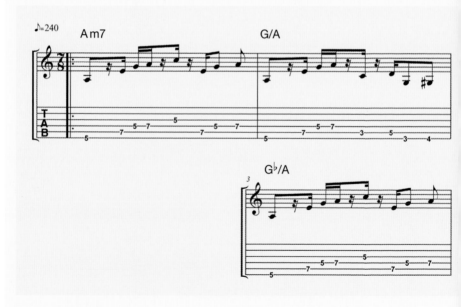

FUSION ODD TIME RIFFS

RIFF REGISTER

Technique: Use alternate sixteenth note picking throughout for an accurate, rhythmic performance.

EDCAG position: Shape 1 A minor pentatonic.

Harmonic content: The four-bar chord progression begins on the tonic chord Am7, with ever-more-dissonant triads being superimposed against the repeated A

minor riff until the final triad (E♭), which is a tritone away from the root.

Guitar settings: Neck pickup with tone rolled off slightly.

Amp settings: Select overdrive channel, with preamp level at around eight o'clock.

Effects: None.

WATCH OUT FOR

GETTING YOUR HEAD AROUND THE 7/8 GROOVE! REMEMBER: THIS IS REALLY A BAR OF 4/4 WITH THE LAST EIGHTH NOTE OMITTED—IT'S MUCH EASIER TO PLAY IF YOU THINK OF IT LIKE THAT.

E♭/A

RIFF NO. 3:

PAT METHENY GROUP STYLE

Pat Metheny is a hugely successful guitarist and composer with a jazzy, liquid, clean tone that is very "easy on the ear." All of his compositions are beautifully crafted; when odd time signatures are used, they are always subtle and musically relevant. This example illustrates his approach perfectly—it's not your usual "obvious" odd time fusion riff. Starting with a bar of 7/4, it reverts back to two bars of 4/4 for the remainder of the riff. The 7/4 bar should be treated just as two bars of 4/4 with the last quarter note omitted. It's a similar concept to the previous odd time riff 7/8 example; just in a longer, quarter note form. This effective technique is great for creating long, hypnotic ostinato figures.

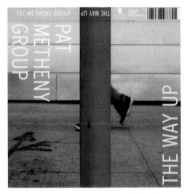

Pat Metheny Group's *The Way Up* (2005).

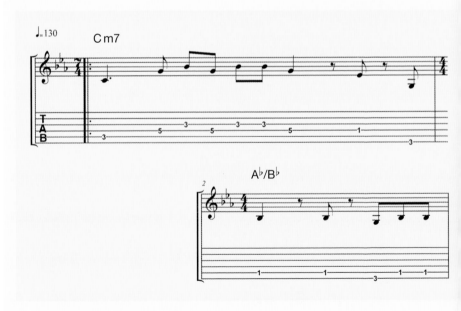

FUSION ODD TIME RIFFS

RIFF REGISTER

Technique: Straightforward alternate eighth note alternate picking.

EDCAG position: Shape 4 (upper notes) and shape 3 (lower notes) of the C minor pentatonic scale.

Harmonic content: By sounding the tonic note (C) only on the first beat of bar 1, a strong resolution is provided on every repeat. Basing notes on the C minor

pentatonic scale helps to affirm the tonal center.

Guitar settings: Neck pickup with tone backed off at least halfway.

Amp settings: Select clean channel, keeping preamp level low and output high.

Effects: None.

WATCH OUT FOR

SHIFTING FROM SHAPE 3 BACK TO SHAPE 4 ON REPEATS: REMAIN IN THIRD POSITION FOR THE FIRST C AND RETURN TO SHAPE 4 ON THE SECOND NOTE (G). BOTH NOTES SHOULD BE FRETTED WITH YOUR THIRD FINGER.

RIFF NO. 4:
BRUFORD STYLE

Bill Bruford's self-titled band was on the cutting edge of the UK's fusion movement during the late 1970s. The virtuoso drummer began his career as the founder member of progressive rock band Yes, later joining King Crimson. The Bruford band represented yet another dramatic change of direction for the drummer, who was exploring jazz fusion for the first time. The lineup featured Allan Holdsworth on guitar (who had already recorded with Soft Machine, Tony Williams Lifetime, and Gong by this early point in his career), and he is only featured on the first two Bruford albums, *Feels Good to Me* (1978) and *One of a Kind* (1979). This fairly heavy riff in 5/4 would have typically been used as the build into a lighter, freer, improvised solo section.

Allan Holdsworth performing in 1982.

FUSION ODD TIME RIFFS

RIFF REGISTER

Technique: Alternate sixteenth picking with subtle palm muting applied as indicated.

EDCAG position: Shape 1 and shape 5 B minor blues scale.

Harmonic content: Although the accompanying keyboard plays B7 chords throughout the riff, the major third (D#) is avoided throughout. Only the minor third (D) is sounded in the riff's conclusion.

Guitar settings: Bridge pickup setting with volume backed off to "clean up" the sound.

Amp settings: Select distortion channel, setting preamp level to eight o'clock.

Effects: None.

WATCH OUT FOR

THE SHIFT TO SHAPE 5 B MINOR PENTATONIC ON THE FOURTH BEAT. USE YOUR THIRD FINGER AS INDICATED TO FRET THE F AND E—THIS WILL KEEP YOUR FIRST FINGER FREE FOR THE LOW A THAT FOLLOWS.

FILL NO. 1:
JEFF BECK STYLE

Jeff Beck is a master of tone and phrasing; he also has an uncanny ability to "make the guitar talk." This undoubtedly accounts for his long and successful career, which has essentially focused on instrumental music since the early 1970s. Whether playing a melody, a lick, or a fill, Mr. Beck never wastes a note. Unusually for a fusion guitar pioneer, he doesn't play lightning-fast phrases, either. This example is a classic, two-bar, question-and-answer phrase that makes full use of the guitar's range. The opening lick—a lyrical, bluesy line that incorporates melodic use of the whammy bar—is answered by a jazzy, arpeggio-based lick high up in twelfth position. It's much easier to play fills in one place of the neck, but always remember that you'll achieve more dramatic results by using the full range of the instrument.

Jeff Beck performing in the 1970s.

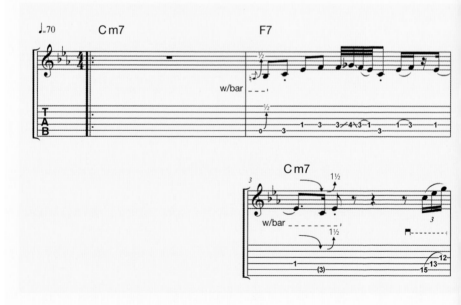

FUSION STYLE FILLS

RIFF REGISTER

Technique: Alternate sixteenth note picking, pitch-accurate whammy bar control, and fast, rhythmic slurs.

EDCAG position: Shape 3 C minor blues scale (first position) and shape 3 C Dorian mode (twelfth position).

Harmonic content: C Dorian mode and Cmin9 arpeggio superimposed over the F7 chord in the second bar. This is a very

melodic way to introduce dominant color tones (that is, ninth, eleventh, and thirteenth).

Guitar settings: Bridge pickup with volume and tone up full.

Amp settings: Select overdrive channel, and set preamp level around seven o'clock.

Effects: None.

WATCH OUT FOR

PLAYING THE OPENING WHAMMY BEND ACCURATELY! DEPRESS THE BAR SLIGHTLY AS YOU PICK THE NOTE—RELEASE THE BAR TO ACHIEVE THAT LIQUID, SYNTH-LIKE SLIDE INTO THE FIRST NOTE.

F7

FILL NO. 2:
JIM MULLEN STYLE

Jim Mullen's intensely melodic improvising technique is based on the principle that an improvised solo is really an improvised melody, not an opportunity to demonstrate technical ability. This approach is nothing new, but it's a concept that many aspiring improvisers overlook. Learning how to phrase your ideas in a musically concise way can improve your soloing technique beyond recognition. It will make your solos appealing to the listener, and that, after all, is the whole point. Super-chops and bags of technique are very impressive, but if they are not used musically they can turn the listener off. Jim Mullen's style also contains plenty of bluesy vocabulary, but because it's always phrased in a jazzy context it never sounds corny—just super-slick and cool.

Jim Mullen performing in 2009.

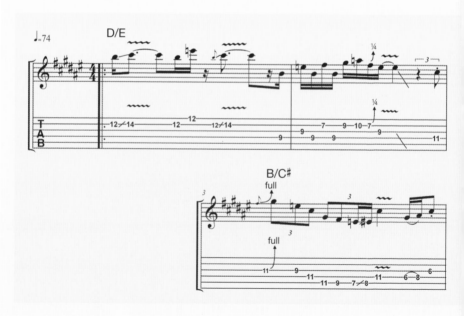

216

RIFF REGISTER

Technique: Can be played entirely with your thumb (using downstrokes) for an authentic tone. However, it's much easier to play using conventional sixteenth note alternate picking.

EDCAG position: Bars 1 and 2: shape 1 E major pentatonic and shape 5 E Mixolydian mode. Bars 2 and 4: shape 1 C# minor pentatonic/Mixolydian mode, and shape 5 C# major pentatonic scales.

Harmonic content: Mixing and matching of the minor blues scale, major pentatonic, and Mixolydian mode allows freedom to incorporate any of the blues tensions/color tones over the shifting eleventh chords.

Guitar settings: Neck pickup with tone rolled off almost completely.

Amp settings: Select clean channel, but drive the amp hard to achieve a "fat" tone.

WATCH OUT FOR

CONFIDENTLY SWITCHING BETWEEN SIXTEENTH NOTE SYNCOPATIONS AND QUARTER NOTE TRIPLETS. LISTEN CAREFULLY TO THE CD TO ENSURE YOU INTERPRET THE PHRASING CORRECTLY.

FILL NO. 3:

MIKE STERN STYLE

Mike Stern took the bebop phrasing of the great horn players, mixed it with established blues guitar vocabulary, dialed in an overdriven rock tone, and created a staggeringly original fusion guitar style. Horn players have used a technique called chromatic encirclement (where the note immediately above and below a note is sounded first) since the days of bebop. This technique does not lend itself to guitar, especially when playing at speed. It's much easier to play thirds or fourths quickly (i.e., the minor pentatonic scale). Stern wasn't the first jazz guitarist to employ this technique, but he was certainly the first player to use multiple instances of it in the same phrase just as the horn players of the bebop era did. Playing sixteenth notes accurately—with unusual fingering patterns—will be challenging, so start this example *slowly*.

Mike Stern performing in 2001.

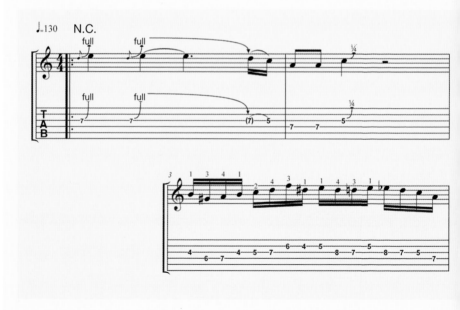

RIFF REGISTER

Technique: Alternate sixteenth note picking. Economy picking can be incorporated where string changes occur, if desired.

EDCAG position: Bars 1 and 2: shape 1 A minor pentatonic. Bars 2 and 3: shape 1 A harmonic minor/A minor blues scale.

Harmonic content: The underlying bass riff implies an Am7 vamp. Chromatic

encirclement is used to highlight the root note (B–G#–A) and the perfect fifth (F–D#–E) of the chord in the fill.

Guitar settings: Neck pickup with volume and tone on full.

Amp settings: Select distortion channel, setting preamp gain at around eight o'clock.

Effects: Stereo chorus and delay pedal.

WATCH OUT FOR

THE UNFAMILIAR FINGERING PATTERN IN BAR 3. USE THE FINGERINGS SUGGESTED IN THE NOTATION FOR BEST RESULTS. NOTICE HOW THE FIRST FINGER PLAYS BOTH THE D# AND E, RETURNING YOUR HAND TO THE MORE FAMILIAR FIFTH POSITION ON BEAT 3.

FILL NO. 4:
PAT METHENY STYLE

The epitome of taste and musicality, Pat Metheny's Grammy award-winning style is never ostentatious—to the casual listener his lead lines blend effortlessly into the music. This example is based on the 7/4 riff previously studied in *Fusion odd time riffs* section (no. 3). Playing a riff in 7/4 is no easy task, but to improvise fluently and musically in this groove presents another set of challenges altogether. If you look closer at the first bar, you'll notice that it has been subdivided into two phrases: the first lasts three beats and the second four beats. This is the best way to approach the problem of soloing in longer time signatures—split each bar into more natural, manageable chunks. However, remember that the concept on its own is not enough: fluency only comes after a lot of practice, just like in every other discipline!

Pat Metheny performing in 2000.

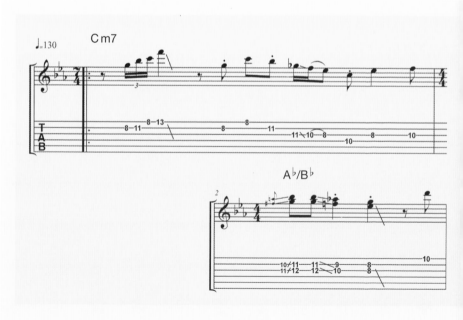

FUSION STYLE FILLS

RIFF REGISTER

Technique: Alternate sixteenth note picking, moving into alternate or "down-up-down" eighth note triplet picking in the final bar.

EDCAG position: Bar 1: shape 1 C minor blues scale. Bars 2 and 3: shape 4 F Dorian mode.

Harmonic content: This is an unresolving VI–V sequence in E♭ major which suggests that C Aeolian mode could be used

throughout. Although it contains exactly the same notes, it's much better to use the F Dorian mode over B♭11 in bars 2 and 3.

Guitar settings: Neck pickup with tone backed off at least halfway.

Amp settings: Select clean channel, keeping preamp level low and output high.

Effects: None.

WATCH OUT FOR

BEING DRAGGED "OUT OF POSITION" DURING THAT LONG, DESCENDING TRIPLET PHRASE. YOU CAN AVOID THIS BY FRETTING THE D ON BEAT 3 WITH A FIRST FINGER STRETCH, REMAINING IN EIGHTH POSITION SO YOU CAN FRET THE REMAINING NOTES WITH EASE.

This section of the book is designed to follow on from Scales & Chops in the previous book of the series, *100 Killer Licks & Chops for Rock Guitar*—that's why there's no information provided on basic scales such as the minor and major pentatonic or the major scale. If you're not already fluent with these scales, it's well worth getting your hands on a copy to get up to speed! To build your essential modal vocabulary, we will be exploring the Dorian mode, Mixolydian mode, Super Locrian mode, and Phrygian dominant mode. These may sound mysterious and exotic, but they are widely used in many genres, especially metal and fusion. Practicing these scales will also advance your technique, harmonic knowledge, and your aural skills—in short, they're guaranteed to make you a better guitar player!

Each mode is presented in five CAGED shapes, and is followed by a section clearly illustrating the corresponding diatonic chords in conventional notation, TAB, and chord box format. These are very useful for writing riffs and modal chord progressions, and will also expand your chord vocabulary. Finally there's a "workout" section for each of the four modes. This section is outlined in detail below, to make your practice sessions more productive and rewarding.

Practice patterns

These have been designed to provide you with greater fluency than traditional ascending and descending patterns. They will help you to really learn each mode inside out—essential for creating licks and fills on the fly. Each mode has its own specific suggested pattern; however, these can (and should) be applied to any other

SCALES AND CHOPS

mode or scale. You should apply each exercise to all five CAGED positions before transposing them and ultimately applying them to all other modes and scales.

Diatonic seventh arpeggio patterns

These four note arpeggios correspond to the diatonic seventh chords of each mode explained in the preceding section. The exercises are designed to improve both your fretting hand fluency and your picking hand control, so it's important to pay attention to the fingerings and picking indications suggested. When using the same finger to play another string on the same fret, you should use a "rolling" movement across the strings—don't waste time and energy lifting it on and off the strings. This efficient approach also prevents notes from sounding simultaneously. In addition, two picking

techniques can also be applied to these exercises: sixteenth note alternate picking and economy picking (the latter is indicated above the TAB). Only attempt economy picking once you are fluent with the fretting hand patterns.

Tempo

Begin with a tempo that's comfortable, and always practice with a metronome. It's really important to start slowly, as you'll build your technique much more efficiently this way. Be patient, and keep a practice log that includes tempo markings so you can keep a record of your progress.

If you apply all of these patterns and techniques to all of the CAGED shapes in all keys, there's enough material here to provide months—even years—of study. What are you waiting for? Grab that guitar and let's get started!

SCALES AND CHOPS
THE DORIAN MODE

Scale type: Seven note, minor.

Parent mode: C major scale.

Scale formula: R–2–♭3–4–5–6–♭7–Oct

Usage: Cool and jazzy tonic minor scale that also sounds great when superimposed over dominant and half-diminished (m7♭5) chords.

Characteristics: The major sixth is the interval that defines this scale, giving it a much brighter sound than its Aeolian mode (natural minor scale) cousin.

Ex 1 D Dorian Mode Shape One

Ex 2 D Dorian Mode Shape Two

Ex 3 D Dorian Mode Shape Three

Ex 4 D Dorian Mode Shape Four

Ex 5 D Dorian Mode Shape Five

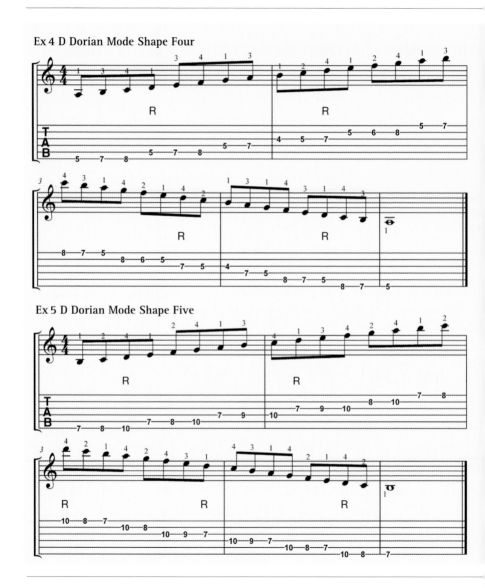

SCALES AND CHOPS
DORIAN MODE DIATONIC CHORDS

Ex 1 Diatonic seventh chords

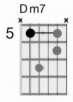 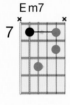 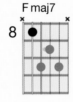

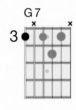 

SCALES AND CHOPS
DORIAN MODE WORKOUT

Ex 1 Diatonic thirds (shape one)

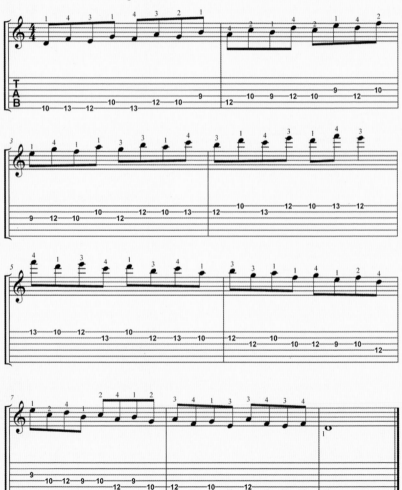

Ex 2 Diatonic 4-note arpeggios (shape one)

(economy picking shown)

SCALES AND CHOPS
THE MIXOLYDIAN MODE

Scale type: Seven note, dominant.

Parent mode: C major scale.

Scale formula: R–2–3–4–5–6–♭7–Oct

Usage: Your first choice for playing over dominant seventh chords. Used in every genre from blues to fusion. Suitable for static dominants (i.e., non-resolving) in major or minor keys, or functioning dominants (resolving) in major keys.

Characteristics: The most "inside"-sounding dominant scale contains benign color tones (major second, perfect fourth, and major sixth), which makes it perfect for complementing resolving dominants in any major key.

Ex 1 G Mixolydian Mode Shape One

Ex 2 G Mixolydian Mode Shape Two

Ex 3 G Mixolydian Mode Shape Three

Ex 4 G Mixolydian Mode Shape Four

Ex 5 G Mixolydian Mode Shape Five

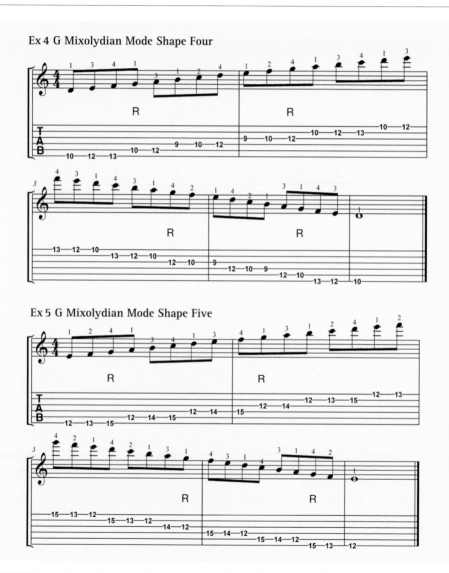

SCALES AND CHOPS

MIXOLYDIAN MODE DIATONIC CHORDS

Ex 1 Diatonic seventh chords

G7 Am7 Bm7(♭5) Cmaj7 Dm7 Em7 Fmaj7

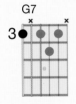

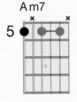

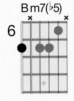

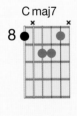

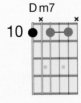

SCALES AND CHOPS
MIXOLYDIAN MODE WORKOUT

Ex 1 Diatonic fourths (shape one)

Ex 2 Diatonic 4-note arpeggios (shape one)

(economy picking shown)

SCALES AND CHOPS
THE SUPER LOCRIAN MODE

Scale type: Seven note, dominant.

Parent mode: A♭melodic minor scale.

Scale formula: R–♭2–♭3–3 – #4–#5–♭7–Oct

Usage: Creates tension over resolving dominant chords in major or minor keys. Can be superimposed over regular dominant chords to intensify resolution in a perfect cadence. N.B. It can be applied to all dominant chords, not just "altered" dominants with #9, ♭9, or #5 extensions.

Characteristics: The most "outside"-sounding dominant scale contains "altered" color tones (also referred to as the "altered scale" for this reason). This dark and exotic scale will add an extra dimension to your fills and solos, but must be resolved carefully.

Ex 1 G Superlocrian Mode Shape One

Ex 2 G Superlocrian Mode Shape Two

Ex 3 G Superlocrian Mode Shape Three

Ex 4 G Superlocrian Mode Shape Four

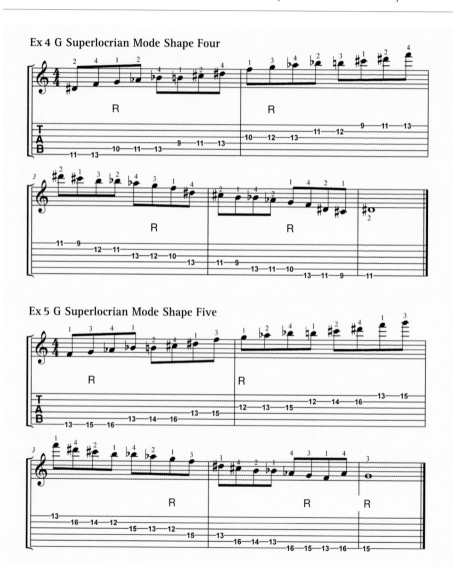

Ex 5 G Superlocrian Mode Shape Five

SCALES AND CHOPS
SUPERLOCRIAN MODE DIATONIC CHORDS

Ex 1 Diatonic seventh chords

G7#5 A♭m(maj7) B♭m7 Bmaj7#5 D♭7 E♭7 Fm7♭5

* The Superlocrian mode is traditionally enharmonised to create a dominant seventh on I, as a result it shares many common tones with the II chord.

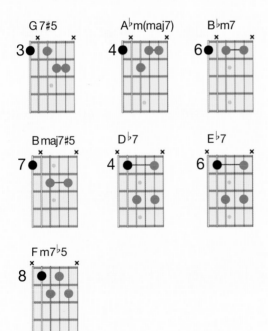

SCALES AND CHOPS
SUPER LOCRIAN MODE WORKOUT

Ex 1 1-4-3-2 linear pattern (shape one)

Ex 2 Diatonic 4-note arpeggios (shape one)

(economy picking shown)

SCALES AND CHOPS
THE PHRYGIAN DOMINANT MODE

Scale type: Seven note, dominant.

Parent mode: C harmonic minor scale.

Scale formula: R–♭2–3–4–5–♭6–♭7–Oct

Usage: Much loved by neoclassical metal guitarists such as Yngwie Malmsteen, this scale is also widely used in jazz and fusion. It's perfect for playing over resolving dominant chords in a minor key.

Characteristics: The minor third interval between the scales' second and third steps mark this scale as a harmonic minor mode. The minor second also adds a distinct Spanish flavor.

Ex 1 G Phrygian Dominant Mode Shape One

Ex 2 G Phrygian Dominant Mode Shape Two

Ex 3 G Phrygian Dominant Mode Shape Three

Ex 4 G Phrygian Dominant Mode Shape Four

Ex 5 G Phrygian Dominant Mode Shape Five

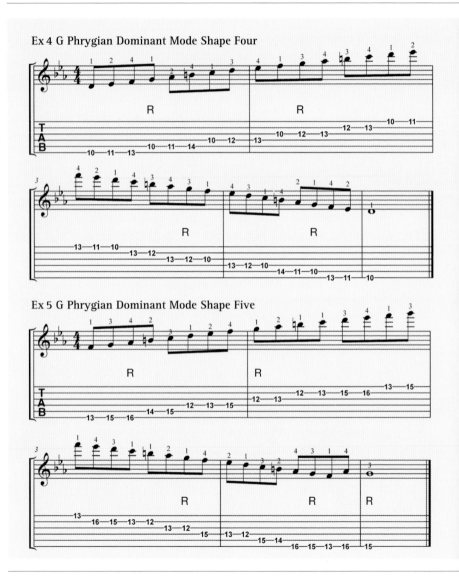

SCALES AND CHOPS
PHRYGIAN DOMINANT MODE DIATONIC CHORDS

Ex 1 Diatonic seventh chords

G7 A♭maj7 B♭dim7 C m(maj7) Dm7b5 E♭maj7#5 F m7

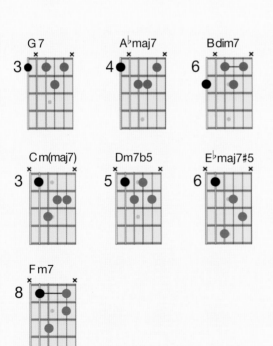

SCALES AND CHOPS
PHRYGIAN DOMINANT MODE WORKOUT

Ex 1 Diatonic fifths (shape one)

Ex 2 Diatonic 4-note arpeggios (shape one)

Blues Rock

1 John Mayall Blues Breakers with Eric Clapton • (aka *The Beano Album*) (1966)
2 Cream • *Disraeli Gears* (1967)
3 Led Zeppelin • *Led Zeppelin II* (1969)
4 Free • *Fire and Water* (1970)
5 Allman Brothers Band • *At Fillmore East* (1971)
6 Mountain • *Nantucket Sleighride* (1971)
7 Rory Gallagher • *Live in Europe* (1972)
8 Stevie Ray Vaughan • *Texas Flood* (1983)
9 Gary Moore • *Still Got the Blues* (1990)
10 Joe Bonamassa • *Sloe Gin* (2007)

Classic Rock

1 Jimi Hendrix • *Electric Ladyland* (1968)
2 Santana • *Abraxas* (1970)
3 The Who • *Who's Next* (1971)
4 The Rolling Stones • *Sticky Fingers* (1971)
5 Deep Purple • *Made in Japan* (1972)
6 Wishbone Ash • *Argus* (1972)
7 Boston • *Boston* (1976)
8 The Eagles • *Hotel California* (1976)
9 Dire Straits • *Dire Straits* (1978)
10 Foreigner • *4* (1981)

Heavy Metal

1 Black Sabbath • *Paranoid* (1970)
2 Led Zeppelin • *Led Zeppelin IV* (1971)
3 Rainbow • *Rising* (1976)
4 Van Halen • *Van Halen* (1978)
5 Ozzy Osbourne • *Blizzard of Ozz* (1980)
6 Iron Maiden • *The Number of the Beast* (1982)
7 Judas Priest • *Screaming for Vengeance* (1982)
8 Metallica • *Master of Puppets* (1986)
9 Guns N' Roses • *Appetite for Destruction* (1987)
10 Megadeth • *Rust in Peace* (1990)

Progressive Rock

1. The Moody Blues • *Days of Future Passed* (1967)
2. King Crimson • *In the Court of the Crimson King* (1969)
3. Yes • *The Yes Album* (1971)
4. Yes • *Close to the Edge* (1972)
5. Pink Floyd • *The Dark Side of the Moon* (1973)*
6. King Crimson • *Larks' Tongues in Aspic* (1973)
7. Mike Oldfield • *Tubular Bells* (1973)
8. Genesis • *Selling England by the Pound* (1973)
9. Emerson, Lake & Palmer • *Brain Salad Surgery* (1973)
10. Rush • *Permanent Waves* (1980)

Alternative Rock

1. Television • *Marquee Moon* (1977)
2. Talking Heads • *Talking Heads:77* (1977)
3. XTC • *Drums and Wires* (1979)
4. The Smiths • *Hatful of Hollow* (1984)
5. Red Hot Chili Peppers • *Blood Sugar Sex Magik* (1991)
6. R.E.M. • *Automatic for the People* (1992)
7. Radiohead • *Pablo Honey* (1993)
8. Green Day • *Dookie* (1994)
9. Muse • *Absolution* (2003)
10. The Strokes • *Room on Fire* (2003)

Fusion

1. Miles Davis • *Bitches Brew* (1970)
2. Mahavishnu Orchestra • *The Inner Mounting Flame* (1971)
3. Billy Cobham • *Spectrum* (1973)
4. Soft Machine • *Bundles* (1975)
5. Jeff Beck • *Wired* (1976)
6. Bruford • *Feels Good to Me* (1978)
7. Mike Stern • *Upside Downside* (1986)
8. Chick Corea • *The Chick Corea Elektric Band* (1986)
9. Pat Metheny Group • *Still Life (Talking)* (1987)
10. Morrissey–Mullen • *Happy Hour* (1988)

EQUIPMENT LIST

Guitarists always love talking and reading about the gear they use. So here's a list of all the guitars and equipment used to create the accompanying CD:

1975 Fender Telecaster

1979 Fender Stratocaster

1980 Rickenbacker 4001 Bass

1982 Gibson ES-335

1986 Steinberger GP4M

1988 Rickenbacker 360 12-string

2004 Fender Jazz Bass

2008 Gibson SG Bass

Wilson Classical Guitar

Johnson steel string acoustic

Mesa Boogie Studio Preamp

Native Instruments Guitar Rig 4

Apple Mac Computers

INDEX

PICTURE CREDITS

All other images are the copyright of Quintet Publishing Ltd. While every effort has been made to credit contributors, Quintet Publishing would like to apologize should there have been any omissions or errors—and would be pleased to made the appropriate correction for future editions of the book.